SHELL EDUCATION

Digital Resources Included

Grades **K–2**

Standards-Based Investigations
Science Labs

Authors

Sue Barford, Faye Glew, Peter Hope, Katrina Housel,
Cheryl Jakab, Mary Rosenberg, Melinda Oldham,
John Pearce, Suzanne Peterson, Judith Sise, and Ormiston Walker

SHELL EDUCATION

Credits

Associate Editor
Josh Roby

Assistant Editor
Leslie Huber, M.A.

Editorial Director
Dona Herweck Rice

Editor-in-Chief
Sharon Coan, M.S.Ed.

Editorial Manager
Gisela Lee, M.A.

Creative Director
Lee Aucoin

Cover Design
Lee Aucoin

Illustration Manager
Timothy J. Bradley

**Interior Layout Design/
Print Production**
Robin Erickson

Publisher
Corinne Burton, M.A.Ed.

Shell Education

5301 Oceanus Drive

Huntington Beach, CA 92649

http://www.shelleducation.com

ISBN 978-1-4258-0163-2

© 2008 Shell Educational Publishing, Inc.

Reprinted 2013

Table of Contents

Table of Contents *(cont.)*

Introduction and Research Base

Why a Focus on Science?

Over three decades ago, the American Association for the Advancement of Science began a three-phase project to develop and promote science literacy: Project 2061. The project was established with the understanding that more is not effective (1989, p. 4).

Inquiry-Based Learning

As Project 2061 began, researchers questioned the appropriateness and effectiveness of science textbooks and methods of instruction. Since textbook instruction puts more emphasis on learning correct answers and less on exploration, collaboration, and inquiry, the Association asserts that this manner of instruction actually "impedes progress toward scientific literacy" (1989, p. 14).

This same concern resurfaced over a decade later by Daniels and Zemelman (2004) who call textbooks "unfriendly." When most adults are choosing literature, they do not pick up their son's or daughter's science textbook. Daniels and Zemelman assert that today's textbooks are best used as reference books when students need large amounts of information on a particular topic within a subject area. Instead, they recommend the use of "authentic" sources.

Project 2061 recommends pedagogical practices where the learning of science is as much about the process as the result or outcome (1989, p. 147). Following the nature of scientific inquiry, students ask questions and are actively engaged in the learning process. They collect data and are encouraged to work within teams of their peers to investigate the unknown. This method of process learning refocuses the students' learning from knowledge and comprehension to application and analysis. Students may also formulate opinions (synthesis and evaluation) and determine whether their processes were effective or needed revision (evaluation).

The National Science Education Standards view inquiry as "central to science learning" (p. 2 of Overview). In this way, students may develop their understanding of science concepts by combining knowledge with reasoning and thinking skills. Kreuger and Sutton (2001) also report an increase in students' comprehension of text when knowledge learning is coupled with hands-on science activities (p. 52).

Values, Attitudes, and Skills

Scientists work under a distinctive set of values. Therefore, according to the American Association for the Advancement of Science, science education should do the same (1989, p. 133). Students whose learning includes data, a testable hypothesis, and predictability in science will share in the values of the scientists they study. Additionally, "science education is in a particularly strong position to foster three [human] attitudes and values: curiosity, openness to new ideas, and skepticism" (1989, p. 134). Science Labs addresses each of these recommendations by engaging students in thought-provoking, open-ended discussions and projects.

Within the recommendations of skills needed for scientific literacy, the American Association for the Advancement of Science suggests attention to computation, manipulation and observation, communication, and critical response. These skills are best learned through the process of learning, rather than in the knowledge itself (1989, p. 135).

Water Cycle

This chapter provides activities that address McREL Science Standard 1.

Student understands atmospheric processes and the water cycle

How to Teach the Water Cycle

Dihydrogen Oxide

Dihydrogen Oxide, AKA H_2O, AKA water, is a familiar material which offers a wealth of opportunities for play and exploration. Students will have seen water in several different forms—liquid water, solid ice, and gaseous steam. Water changes state easily, back and forth, from one form to another. Other materials do the same—wax and chocolate, for example. But only water easily offers all three states—solid, liquid, and gas—in our everyday experience. And it's never possible to get the wax and chocolate back just the way they were!

Water

Water is the liquid state of the material. Liquid water is essential for life. Liquid water takes the shape of the container in which you put it, whether it be a bucket, cup, or jug. It flows downhill, but it won't go up except in a flood (although you can make a continuous column of water flow over and down if you use a siphon). Students will have had a lot of experience with water and its qualities in the bath, swimming pool, and ice cube tray.

Ice

Ice is the solid form of water. It is formed when pure water drops in temperature below 0°C (32°F). An amazing quality of water is that it expands as it freezes—tops are pushed off milk bottles and car radiators can be cracked. Frozen water takes up more space than it did as a liquid. As a result, the ice is less dense than water—the same amount of mass in a larger volume.

Steam

Strictly speaking, the billowing clouds that come from a boiling kettle are water vapor. Steam itself—water in its gaseous state—is invisible. You can see where it is by looking carefully at the spout of a boiling kettle—you can just see a clear space between the spout and the vapor. This invisible gas is true steam.

The stuff that fills the bathroom, making condensation run down the cold mirror and windows, is water vapor—liquid water in tiny droplets. It condenses on cold surfaces. This process is called condensation, and the liquid that condenses is called condensed water. However, if you tell your neighbors that you are having trouble with condensed water on your double-glazing, they may think you're a bit of a show off.

Lighter than Water

Water particles bonded together make ice. Unfortunately for the *Titanic*, ice is lighter than water. This is a very unusual but important fact that comes up time and again in this book. It is very unusual for a solid material to weigh less than its liquid. Apart from water, only a material called bismuth behaves like this. (You might have come across this pinkish metal if you have had a gastric ulcer. It is used in soothing medicines.)

Once you understand particle theory, you can understand why this should be. When water freezes, its particles form a kind of cage—a rigid pattern in which the particles are held away from each other. So there is more space in an ice cube than there is in water.

Where Does Rain Come From?

Rainwater isn't new. It's been round and round the water cycle forever. All of Earth's water is trapped in this endless cycle of change. When you drink a glass of water, you can be fairly sure that at

How to Teach the Water Cycle *(cont.)*

least one of the molecules at one time was part of the water drunk by a hero of yours, or by a historical character.

It's statistically likely. It has been estimated that a molecule of water from a glass poured into the sea at New York will wash up on the beach in California in a matter of months. On the way, it will have had amazing adventures—as part of the sea, a pond, a river, a cup of tea, or a glass of cola.

You don't have to look far to see examples of the water cycle all around you. Consider, for example, getting caught out in the rain. When you get home, you take off your wet clothes and put them in the washing machine. By the time you have done this, the weather has brightened up, and you hang the clothes outside to dry. The water returns to the sky. These simple actions demonstrate a simple water cycle. While the basic story of the water cycle is the same, the variations are enormous.

Water Evaporates

Molecules of water close to the surface are in constant movement. If they have enough energy, they break free of the water and lift into the sky. This can happen at any time. If you leave a saucer of water on a windowsill, meaning to put a potted plant in it later, the water will evaporate at room temperature. By the time you put the potted plant there a day or two later, the water level will have dropped. The water is evaporating.

Evaporation happens much faster if you put a bit of energy into the system. If you heat the water, the molecules get excited and break off with far more regularity. The water may "steam." It loses water molecules fast and if you are not careful, it will boil dry. The more energy you apply, the faster the evaporation. Boiling water is losing molecules fast. While they are above boiling point, the water molecules are actually a gas—water gas.

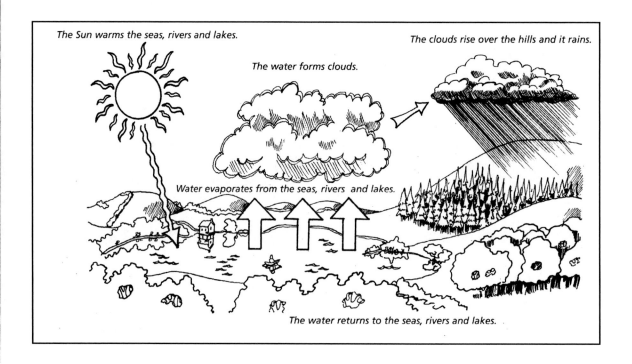

The Sun warms the seas, rivers and lakes.

The water forms clouds.

The clouds rise over the hills and it rains.

Water evaporates from the seas, rivers and lakes.

The water returns to the seas, rivers and lakes.

How to Teach the Water Cycle *(cont.)*

What's in a Cloud?

You have probably flown through a cloud if you have flown in an airplane. But you have also walked through one if you have seen mist or fog on the ground. Both clouds and mist are made up of water vapor, condensed into minute water particles that float in the atmosphere or roll across the hills.

As the water vapor rises, it cools, and it clumps or condenses, often around tiny dust particles. The smog of the big cities is caused by water condensing around waste from fires or car exhaust.

The cloudiness of water vapor is what makes it hard to see on misty days. If there is a fair amount of water vapor in the air, it is hard to see great distances. When you visit a hot, dry country, you may be astonished by the clarity of distant things and the sharpness of the colors. There is little water vapor in the air to spoil your view.

So the water cycle starts when the water around us—in the seas, rivers, streams, ponds, swimming pools, and even in that dish on the windowsill—evaporates from the surface and rises into the sky, to form clouds.

There's a big role for trees here, as they pull water from the ground and lose it through their leaves—a process known as transpiration.

A handy spin-off of this evaporation process is that the water that rises into the atmosphere is clean. It has left all its impurities behind. There are even rings of impurity left on that saucer. The pure water has gone up to form clouds.

Down Came the Rain

Clouds are unstable. As they rise and cool, the water condenses. Droplets run together to form bigger and bigger drops. Finally, these drops are so big that they can no longer hang in the air, and they fall as rain.

Condensing is the process of combining the water molecules. You see it taking place in your bathroom. Reaching a cold surface, water vapor from your shower condenses into water droplets, and these run down the mirror or window. We call these droplets (incorrectly) condensation. In fact, it is condensed water. It's the process that is condensation.

Up in the clouds, the condensed water droplets start to fall. Because this usually happens at quite a height, it is more likely to occur in mountainous or hilly places, or close to them.

If clouds are carried by the wind over high ground, they may rise higher and higher, getting colder and colder. The water vapor freezes. (Snow is frozen vapor, not frozen liquid.) and a crystal of ice is formed in these high clouds. As updrafts push the clouds higher still, more water vapor joins the crystals, and when they are too heavy to be suspended any longer, they fall as snow. If more water gathers around the frozen particle, it forms a hailstone.

Rivers and Streams

Once it has fallen as rain, the water's journey is far from over. Many possibilities arise. A droplet of rain may join a stream or river. It may soak into the ground, only to pop up somewhere else in a spring or well. It may scarcely touch the earth, hardly arriving before it evaporates away again.

Or it may start a long adventure that includes pushing a turbine around to generate electricity, being boiled for a

---

How to Teach the Water Cycle *(cont.)*

cup of tea, passing through one or more humans, being cleaned in a sewage treatment plant, falling through a shower head, and being mixed with lemonade mix. It may wash your car, water your garden, or boil your potatoes. It may be drawn into a plant and combined with oxygen to produce more plant material and food for animals. Eventually, it may find itself back in the sea. And the whole cycle begins again.

A drop of water may travel thousands of kilometers between the time it evaporates and the time it falls to earth again as rain or snow. On the way, it may be partly responsible for some extreme weather conditions.

Storms

Thunderstorms are heavy storms with rain, thunder, and lightning. We usually get them in the summer because then the ground gets hot, and the rising warm air forms tall clouds with a flat "anvil" top. Electricity crackles in these clouds, caused by water particles rubbing together. When the charge has built up, it snaps to the ground as a flash of lightning. The air heated by the lightning flash creates shock waves that we hear as thunder.

Lightning travels at 140,000 km per second. That's half the speed of light. While the streak is very narrow (less than two cm wide), it can be 43 km long. You can survive being hit by lightning as long as it goes to Earth without passing through your heart. Park ranger Roy Sullivan claimed to have been hit by lightning seven times between 1942 and 1977.

Counting the seconds between flash and bang can give you an idea of the distance between you and a storm. Allow three seconds for a kilometer and five seconds for a mile.

Thunderclouds can grow to be 15–20 km high. Their anvil shape is caused by high winds at that height, blowing the top sideways. Some of the water in them stays unfrozen, even at minus 40°C. But clouds also contain fragments of ice that are growing onion-like, layer by layer. They then may become too heavy to be held up by currents of air and so fall to the ground as hail. If the air currents are really fast (as much as 145 kph), the hailstones may grow to the size of oranges before they drop from the cloud.

Hurricanes and Tornadoes

A hurricane (called a typhoon in the Northern Pacific and a cyclone in the Indian Ocean) originates close to the equator when a central calm eye is surrounded by inwardly spiraling winds. As the sea temperature rises, water evaporates into whirling, unstable storm clouds. A hurricane is a wind of force 12 or more on the Beaufort scale and is accompanied by lightning and torrential rain. Hurricane Gilbert in the Caribbean in 1988 gusted up to 320 kph. A cyclone in the Bay of Bengal in November 1970 caused the sea to rise ten meters, crashing into the Ganges delta to drown at least 300,000 people and one million farm animals.

The Seasons

Earth is going around the Sun. The time it takes to complete a full orbit—365 and a quarter days—we call a year.

Earth's axis is at a slight angle to the Sun. This angle stays the same as Earth orbits the Sun. Any point on Earth's surface will spend some of the year leaning towards the Sun and in strong sunlight. This is summer in this part of Earth. It will spend some of the year leaning away from the Sun, and then it will be winter in this part of Earth.

How to Teach the Water Cycle *(cont.)*

Daylight hours are longer in the summer and shorter in the winter. Between the summer and the winter is spring, when daylight hours get longer and it gets warmer, and autumn, when daylight hours get shorter and it gets colder. On one day in the spring and one in autumn, day and night are exactly the same length. These days are called the equinoxes.

Daylight Times

In the summer, the Sun shines early in the morning. The evenings are long and children play outside until quite late. You may even go to bed while it is still light outside. Then in the winter, daylight time is shorter. The mornings are dark and you spend the evenings indoors.

Earth is tilted as it orbits the Sun. In the summer, the Sun appears in the sky for longer and climbs higher. In the winter, the Sun appears in the sky for a shorter time and does not climb so high. The changes in daylight time follow a pattern, and it is possible to predict this pattern to the minute.

Here are some sunrise and sunset times for London in the month of June 2000. The sunrise times are the time to the minute that the Sun rose. So on June 8, 2000, the Sun rose at 4:44 in the morning—nearly a quarter to five. The sunset times are the times the Sun set. So on June 8, 2000, the Sun set at 20:14 (8:14 at night), or nearly a quarter past eight.

Date	Sunrise	Sunset
1st	04:48 a.m.	8:08 p.m.
8th	04:44 a.m.	8:14 p.m.
15th	04:42 a.m.	8:19 p.m.
22nd	04:43 a.m.	8:21 p.m.
29th	04:47 a.m.	8:20 p.m.

How Can I Make a Thermometer?

Name _____

What You Need:
- water
- rubbing alcohol
- plastic water bottle
- food coloring
- drinking straw
- modeling clay

What To Do:

1. Watch your teacher fill the bottle about halfway full with equal parts of water and rubbing alcohol.

2. Add food coloring to the water and rubbing alcohol mixture.

3. Place the straw in the bottle making sure the straw does not touch the bottom of the bottle.

4. Use the modeling clay to seal the top of the bottle closed and to hold the straw in place.

5. Place your hands around the bottle and tell the rest of the class what happens.

6. Pass the bottle around and have each classmate place his or her hands around the bottle to see what happens.

DO NOT DRINK THE WATER AND RUBBING ALCOHOL MIXTURE.

 Next Question

What happens to the water and rubbing alcohol mixture as it is heated and cooled? How could you make the water bottle into a working thermometer?

 Notebook Reflection

Describe the experiment in your science notebook. Be careful to record your observations. Use drawings as well as words.

What Makes a Tornado?

Name _____

What You Need:
- 2 one-liter soda bottles
- rubber washer the same size as the bottle opening
- electrical tape
- water
- food coloring (optional)

What To Do:

1. Fill one of the bottles 2/3 full of water. If you want, add food coloring to the water.

2. Tape the sides of the washer over the mouth of the bottle. Be sure NOT to cover the hole in the middle of the washer.

3. Place the second bottle on top of the washer. (The tops of the bottles are touching each other.)

4. Use electrical tape to fasten the bottles together.

5. Turn the bottles over. Hold the empty bottom bottle still while rapidly moving the top bottle in circles.

6. Let the bottles go. What happens?

 **Next Question**

Pretend you are stuck in the middle of the bottle tornado. What can you do to survive?

 Notebook Reflection

Describe what happened to the water in this experiment.

Where Does Rain Come From?

Name _____

What You Need:
- ice (one cup of water frozen)
- clear transparent wrap
- measuring cup
- rubber band
- tall, clear drinking glass
- clean sheets of writing paper

What To Do:

1. Watch your teacher set out one cup of ice. Write or draw what you think will happen to the ice. How much water will there be?

2. Once the ice has melted, carefully measure the amount of liquid left behind.

3. Pour the water into the drinking glass. Cover the glass with a piece of transparent wrap. Use the rubber band to keep the clear transparent wrap secured in place. What do you notice happens to the water as time passes?

 **Next Question**

How much water is in the drinking glass? What makes you think that? What would happen if the water in the drinking glass were frozen? How much water would there be?

 Notebook Reflection

What would life be like if water stayed in only one form, solid ice, water, or vapor, and NEVER changed to another form?

Where Does Frost Come From?

Name _____

What You Need:
- 2 or 3 ice cubes
- cold water
- salt
- a tin can
- spoon

What To Do:

1. Place your ice cubes in the tin can.

2. Add just enough water to cover the ice cubes.

3. Put a pinch of salt in the water.

4. Stir for two minutes.

5. Draw what you see on the outside of the can.

6. Feel the outside of your can. Is it hot or cold? _____

_____

7. Is the frost wet or dry? _____

_____

Where Does Frost Come From? *(cont.)*

What To Do: *(cont.)*

8. Place a finger on the can for 20 seconds. Lift your finger.
What happened? Draw what you see.

9. Moist air freezes on things that are cold and solid. This is
called frost. What time of year do you see frost? _____

_____

 **Next
Question**

*What happens when you
sprinkle salt on the frost?*

 **Notebook
Reflection**

*Weather changes every day. Draw
pictures of two other kinds of
weather. Next to each picture,
write the season when you see that
weather the most.*

Where Does Water Go?

Name _____

What You Need:
- two clear 250 mL (8 oz.) cups
- marker
- measuring cup
- ruler
- foil square
- window

What To Do:

1. Add 60 mL (1/4 cup) of water to each cup.

2. Mark the water level on the outside of each cup.

3. Cover one cup with foil.

4. Put the cups in the window.

5. Wait three days.

6. Draw what both cups look like. Be sure to draw the line for the water level on each cup.

What To Do: *(cont.)*

7. Measure the height of the lines.

Cup One Distance: _____

Cup Two Distance: _____

8. Look at the second line. Where is it? Circle one.

Cup with foil: above first line / below first line

Cup without foil: above first line / below first line

9. In the cup without the foil, some of the water left the cup. Where did it go? _____

_____

10. In the cup with the foil, the lid _____

the water vapor in the cup.

 ## Next Question

Why did you put the cups in a spot that had sunlight? What happens when the cups are put in a closet?

 ## Notebook Reflection

Imagine you and your class were water molecules in the cups. Describe what happens when you are left out in the sun.

How Does the Weather Change?

Name _____

What You Need: • an outdoor thermometer

What To Do:

1. Look out the window in the morning.
2. Decide on symbols for each kind of weather. Draw what you see in the chart.
3. Put the thermometer outside. Write the temperature in the chart.

Key: Cloudy   Sunny   Windy   Snow   Rain   Stormy

	Monday	Tuesday	Wednesday	Thursday	Friday
Morning Weather					
Morning Temperature (°C)					
Afternoon Weather					
Afternoon Temperature (°C)					

How Does the Weather Change? *(cont.)*

What To Do: *(cont.)*

4. On what days did the weather change between the morning and the afternoon?

_____

5. How did it change?

_____

6. Between which days of the week did the weather change the most?

_____

7. Was this week mostly hot or cold? _____

8. At what time of day is the temperature usually warmest?

_____

 **Next Question**

Listen to a weather forecast. Write it down. Then watch the weather. Was the forecast right? How do you think people make forecasts?

Look at your chart. Did the weather stay the same each day? Did it change?

 Notebook Reflection

Look at your weather chart from another month. Which month was colder? Is the usual weather the same or different between each month? Do these changes happen every year?

When Does the Sun Rise?

Name _____

What You Need: • newspaper weather sections for five consecutive days

What To Do:

1. Each day, look in the weather section to find when the sun rises and sets. Add the data to the chart below.

	Sunrise	Sunset
Day 1		
Day 2		
Day 3		
Day 4		
Day 5		

2. What season is it? _____

3. What do you notice about the sunrise times? _____

_____

4. What do you notice about the sunset times?

_____

 **Next Question**

Will the times be the same during other seasons? How can you find out?

 Notebook Reflection

Think about the summer. Then think about the winter. Describe how long the days feel.

How Strong Is the Wind?

Name _____

What You Need:
- scissors
- tape
- glue
- cardboard box
- drinking straw
- paper
- metal foil
- 30 cm (1 ft.) light galvanized wire
- parent or relative with a car

What To Do:

1. Make two holes near one edge of the cardboard box, on opposite sides of the box.

2. Push the drinking straw through both holes.

3. Pass the wire through the straw. There should be 15–20 cm (4–6 in.) of wire sticking out both sides.

4. Bend one end of the wire down so it almost reaches across the box.

5. Cut out a cardboard triangle and color it. Tape it to the bent end of the wire.

6. Cut out a rectangle of foil. Fold one edge over the unbent side of the wire. Glue the wire into the crease.

7. Cut a large quarter circle out of the paper. Glue it to the box so the bent wire points down one side of the paper.

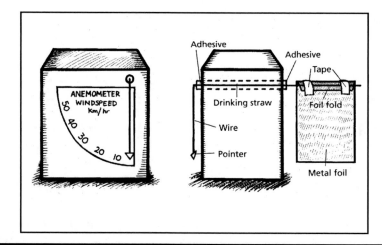

How Strong Is the Wind? *(cont.)*

What To Do: *(cont.)*

8. Label where the triangle points as "0."

9. Ask your parent or guardian to help you calibrate your wind meter. Have them take you for a drive on a calm day. Hold the wind meter out the window so the wind hits the foil.

10. Mark where the arrow points at 10 kph, 20 kph, 30 kph, 40 kph, 50 kph, and 60 kph (5 mph, 10 mph, 15 mph, 20 mph, 25 mph, 30 mph).

11. Now when it is windy, you can use your wind meter to find out how fast the wind is. Hold the wind meter out so the wind hits the foil. The arrow will point to how strong the wind is.

 **Next Question**

Measure the wind in three places on three days. What results do you get?

 **Notebook Reflection**

Why does driving in the car let you calibrate the wind meter?

How Can I Make Rain?

Name _____

What You Need:
- a large glass jar with lid
- small rocks to cover the bottom of the jar
- potting soil
- several small plants
- small jar lid
- water

What To Do:

1. Cover the bottom of the jar with rocks.

2. Add enough potting soil to the jar to create a 10 cm (4 inch) layer of soil.

3. Place the plants in the soil.

4. Water the soil until it is moist.

5. Fill the small jar lid with water and put it in between the plants. This will become a "pond."

6. Put the lid on the jar.

7. Place the jar in a spot where it will get plenty of light but is out of direct sunlight.

 **Next Question**

Pretend you are 2.54 cm (1 in.) tall and live in the terrarium. What else would you need in order to survive?

 Notebook Reflection

Draw a picture of the terrarium. Label the parts of the water cycle modeled in the terrarium: evaporation, condensation, precipitation.

What Happens When Ice Melts?

Name _____

What You Need:
- clear plastic cup
- 1 ice cube
- water
- marker

What To Do:

1. Put an ice cube in your cup. The teacher will fill your cup with water. Draw a line on the cup to show how full it is.

2. Now draw it here:

3. Does the ice float or sink?

   _____

4. Draw the ice. Show how much of the ice is below the water.

What Happens When Ice Melts? *(cont.)*

 What To Do: *(cont.)*

5. The ice will melt. What do you think will happen to the water level?

_____

6. Watch the cup as the ice melts. Compare the water level to the line you drew. Did the water go up or down?

_____

7. Draw the water in the cup after the ice melts.

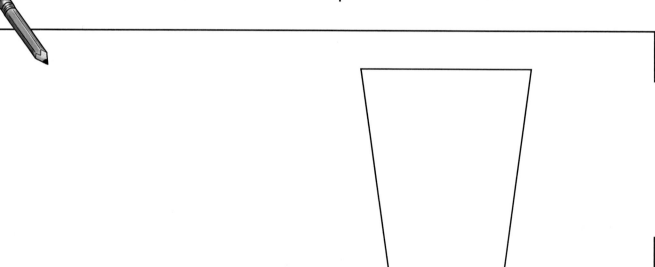

8. Compared to the water, the ice took up_____.

Circle One: more space / less space / same amount

 **Next Question**

Put your cup in the freezer for one hour. What happens to the water?

Is the ice above or below the line you drew on the cup?

 Notebook Reflection

Why did the ice melt? If you put the cup in the freezer, what would happen to the ice? What would happen to the water?

How Much Water Is in Ice?

Name _____

What You Need:
- plastic resealable bag
- water
- sticker
- marker
- measuring cup

What To Do:

1. Measure 100 mL (1/2 cup) of water. Pour the water into a plastic bag. Close the bag.

2. Draw the water in your bag.

3. Write your name on a sticker. Put the sticker on the bag.

4. Put your bag in the freezer. Wait two hours.

5. Take the bag from the freezer. Draw what is in the bag.

What To Do: *(cont.)*

6. Set the bag on your desk. Wait two hours.

7. Draw what's in your bag now.

8. Unzip a part of the bag. Carefully pour the water back into the measuring cup.

How much water is in the measuring cup? _____

Was any water lost as it changed to ice? _____

Was any water lost as the ice changed to water? _____

Where did the ice come from? _____

 Next Question

Take a plastic bottle. Pour your water into it. Will the amount of ice stay the same? How does the shape of the bottle affect the ice?

Notebook Reflection

Where do you see ice in nature? Where does this ice come from?

Geology

This chapter provides activities that address McREL Science Standard 2.

Student understands Earth's composition and structure.

Knows that Earth materials consist of solid rocks, soils, liquid water, and the gases of the atmosphere	What Is the World Made Of?, page 34 How Are Crystals Made?, page 35 How Powerful Is Air?, page 37 Which is Bigger: Hot Air or Cold Air?, page 39
Knows that rocks come in many different shapes and sizes (e.g., boulders, pebbles, sand)	What's Inside a Pebble?, page 41 How Can I Group Rocks?, page 42

How to Teach Geology

Is Soil Made from Dinosaur Droppings?

We live on a rocky planet. Wherever we are, even in the middle of the ocean, there are rocks beneath our feet. These rocks were formed as Earth began to cool.

That cooling process is far from over. Under the hard, cold crust of Earth, the mantle and core of the planet are still intensely hot. They are so hot that molten rock periodically bursts through the crust as volcanoes.

Much of the rock on Earth's surface was formed from this original material, the so-called igneous rocks. But some have been eroded, transported, and laid down in layers of sediment (sedimentary rocks). Some of these have been subjected to intense heat and pressure and have changed or metamorphosed (metamorphic rocks).

Rocks are constantly being broken down. The final product of this breakdown is soil or "earth." Unlike the student who guessed that earth was made of dinosaur droppings, we know that soil is a rich, complex material.

Beneath Our Feet

Earth is like a giant soft-boiled egg. Earth's core—the yolk of the egg—is incredibly hot and liquid. Earth's mantle—the white of the egg—surrounds it and is also hot and liquid. It breaks out in places as volcanoes.

Earth's crust—the shell of the egg—is cold and hard. It is made from solid rock. Wherever you are on Earth, even if you are on a ship in the middle of the sea, there is rock beneath you. You are on solid ground.

Just a minute. The school field isn't rock, nor is the park or the garden. That's because the rock is covered with a layer of earth or soil. If you dig down through this soil, you will find rock under it. Everywhere.

Plate Tectonics

About 200 million years ago, the landmasses of Earth were together as one supercontinent. This single landmass was called Pangea. We also know that the hot, molten magma under the surface of the crust pushed the lands apart. And this motion continues today!

The mid-ocean ridge is a huge underwater mountain range. It has a large crack running down its center. That crack is in Earth's crust. It allows molten magma to seep up. When magma reaches the surface, it is called lava. The lava cools and forms new rock on the ocean floor.

Molten magma rises to the surface through cracks in Earth's crust. This makes new crust. Does that mean there is more crust on the surface of Earth now than in the past? No. Geologists had a theory. If Earth oozed molten magma in one place, then it must reabsorb crust somewhere else.

Sure enough, studies began to show that the Atlantic Ocean floor is expanding. But the Pacific Ocean floor is shrinking. It was found that the Pacific Ocean floor dives down into deep trenches under continents. These trenches are called subduction zones. The expanding and shrinking ocean floors are an example of how Earth is really a recycler. Rocks are created and later recycled.

There are two basic types of plates on Earth. Oceanic plates are under the ocean water. Continental plates make up

How to Teach Geology *(cont.)*

the continents. Plates have three main types of boundaries, or edges. They are divergent, convergent, and transform.

- Divergent boundaries are where two plates move away from each other.

- Convergent boundaries are where two plates crash into each other.

- Transform boundaries are where two plates slide past each other.

Each boundary behaves in a different way. The different boundaries can be found all over the world. The boundaries also make land features such as mountains and valleys.

Divergent Boundaries

Iceland is a tiny island made from the divergent boundary of the mid-ocean ridge. Two plates are moving away from each other very slowly. They move at a rate of two to four centimeters per year.

Volcanoes are common on the island nation of Iceland. The movement of the plates causes magma to burst up and through Earth's crust. This action forms volcanoes. The cooled material from the volcanic eruptions formed the island.

Convergent Boundaries

Plates can form convergent boundaries in one of three ways. Each type of convergent boundary has its own results.

An ocean-ocean collision happens between two ocean plates. Right now, such a collision is causing the Mariana Trench. The fast-moving Pacific Plate is crashing into the Philippine Plate. As the Pacific Plate dives into Earth's mantle, it is melted. This causes earthquakes and volcanoes. The Mariana Islands were made in this way.

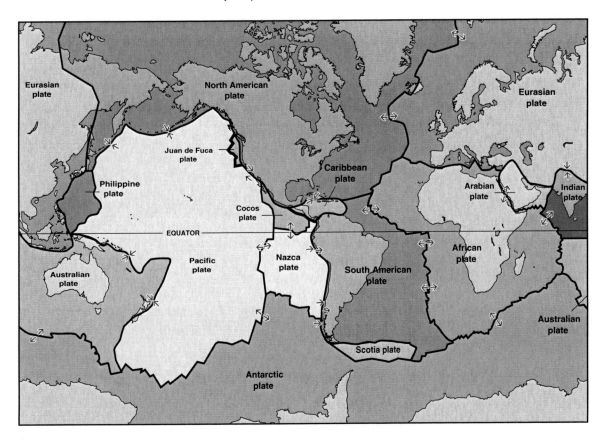

An ocean-continental collision is happening in South America right now. An oceanic plate is being subducted under a continental plate. This is happening near Peru and Chile. That is why earthquakes and volcanoes are very common in this area of the world.

In a continent-continent collision, two plates collide head-on. They "fight it out" before one plate finally subducts under the other. A lot of material builds up as it is scraped off one plate before it subducts. The Himalayas are the highest mountains in the world. They are the result of a collision that started about 50 million years ago. The Indian and Eurasian continental plates crashed together to form the very tall mountain range.

Transform Boundaries

The San Andreas fault in California is a transform boundary. It falls between the Pacific Plate and the North American Plate. These two plates are sliding past each other instead of colliding into each other. This sliding motion has caused major earthquakes in California all along the state. Most transform boundaries are found in the ocean, but the San Andreas fault is on land.

Where Soil Comes From

The weather transforms rocks. Remember we talked about the fact that water expands when it freezes? Well, even the strongest rock can be split by the "ice wedge"—water entering cracks in the rock, freezing, expanding, and splitting the rock apart. Smaller rocks are acted on by wind and rain, the sea, or plant or animal action. Finally, they break down to tiny particles which, mixed with organic matter from plants or animals, make up our soil. Soil is important to plant growth, of course. And plant roots are important for securing the soil against weathering.

A Soil Profile

We are always digging up the ground. We dig holes to build houses and roads and to lay pipes and cables. If there is some digging near you, you might be able to visit it with a class or a group. Stand somewhere safe. Look into the hole that has been dug. You will see the soil profile.

- Topsoil: dark, rich, and full of rotting plants
- Subsoil: different in color; tightly-packed soil
- Rocky soil: a layer of rock that is breaking down to become soil
- Bedrock: this is the rock beneath the soil

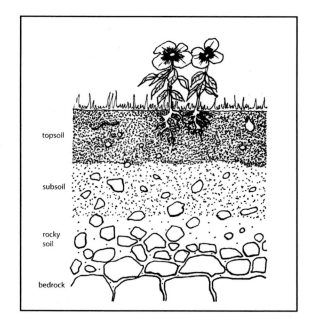

From Rock to Soil

But where does all this soil come from?

Rock is hard, but when the sun shines on it in the day, it swells up. When it is cold at night, it shrinks away. All this swelling and shrinking causes bits to break off. In the middle of winter, cracks fill up with water. The water freezes and the ice begins to push the rock apart. The ice splits the rock open. The river that sweeps past it bangs rocks against it, knocking off chips of rock.

Eventually, the rock crumbles to stone. The stones are rubbed and banged together by the river. The stones become gravel, then grains of sand, and then a fine powder. The powder becomes mixed with bits of rotting plants, living bacteria, tiny fungi that live off the rotting plants, trapped air, and water. The rock becomes soil.

Fascinating Fossils

Fossils are evidence of past life. They are the remains or imprints of living things from long ago. They can be leaf prints, footprints, shell prints, or skeleton prints. The waste from living things can even become fossils!

Fossils are made in different ways. They can be made when a living thing dies and becomes buried by sediments, such as ash from a volcano, mud, sand, or silt. They can be frozen in ice. They can be mummies, too. Some fossils have been buried in tar for thousands of years.

Most fossils are made when the soft parts of a living thing decay. The hard parts are turned into something like rock. The minerals in the sediments seep into the hard parts of the living thing. They become preserved as fossils. Other fossils are made when the whole living thing is frozen or mummified. Then, the soft parts are included, too.

Fossils are more likely to be made when a living thing dies near a body of water than on dry land. Near water, it is likely to be quickly buried. Over thousands of years, the sediments settle into layers that become sedimentary rock. Fossils are often found in sedimentary rock.

What Is the World Made Of?

Name _____

What You Need:
- one liter soda bottle
- a balloon
- vinegar (a liquid)
- baking soda (a solid)
- a funnel

What To Do:

1. Place the funnel in the opening of the liter bottle.

2. Carefully pour the vinegar into the bottle until the base of the bottle is filled.

3. Rinse and dry the funnel and insert it into the balloon.

4. Carefully fill the balloon halfway full with baking soda.

5. Slip the balloon over the opening of the bottle being careful not to allow any of the baking soda to mix with the vinegar.

6. Hold the balloon upright and see what happens!

 **Next Question**

What combination of baking soda and vinegar would make the balloon expand the most?

 Notebook Reflection

What happened when the vinegar and baking soda were mixed? What form of matter was made? How long was the balloon able to stay upright?

How Are Crystals Made?

Name _____

What You Need:
- pencil
- string
- clear plastic cups
- 20 mL (4 tsp.) salt
- 20 mL (4 tsp.) water
- 20 mL (4 tsp.) laundry bluing
- magnifying glass or hand lens

What To Do:

1. Tie the string around the middle of the pencil. Place the pencil across the top of the cup so that the string hangs down into the cup. (The string should touch the bottom of the cup.)

2. In a separate cup, mix together the salt, water, and laundry bluing. Slowly pour the mixture into the cup with the pencil and the string.

3. Use the magnifying glass to see what happens!

4. Place the cup in a sunny window. How big will the crystals become? _____

5. Draw how the crystals change over several days.

Day 1	Day 2

How Are Crystals Made (cont.)

What To Do: (cont.)

5. Draw how crystals change over several days (cont.)

Day 3	Day 4

Day 5

? Next Question

What would happen if a swimming pool were filled with a mixture of water, bluing, and salt?

Notebook Reflection

What happened to the liquid that was poured into the cup? What caused the mixture to bubble?

How Powerful Is Air?

Name _____

What You Need: • a big bowl

• 250 mL (1 c.) clear plastic cup

• water

What To Do:

1. Fill the bowl with water.

2. Put your cup under the water's surface. Let some water flow in.

3. Turn the cup upside down.

4. Lift your cup slowly. Do not lift the rim above the water.

Draw what happens:

What To Do: *(cont.)*

5. Now lift your cup above the top of the water. Is it easy or hard to do?

_____

6. Draw what happens:

7. Gravity is pulling down on the water in the cup. Air pressure on the water in the bowl pushes the water up. So air pressure is _____ than gravity.

Circle One: stronger / weaker

8. You _____ see air.

Circle One: can / cannot

Next Question

What happens if you use a straw instead of a cup?

What happens when you put your finger over the dry end of the straw?

Notebook Reflection

What did you learn about air? Draw a picture of the experiment. Tell what happened.

Which Is Bigger: Hot Air or Cold Air?

Name _____

What You Need:
- one-liter soda bottle
- balloon
- deep bowl
- hot water
- cold water
- ice

What To Do:

1. Stretch out the balloon.

2. Pull the neck of the balloon over the mouth of the bottle.

3. Add hot water to the bowl. Fill the bowl halfway.

4. Hold the bottle with its bottom in the water. Wait three minutes.

5. Draw the bottle and balloon:

Which Is Bigger: Hot Air or Cold Air? *(cont.)*

What To Do: *(cont.)*

6. Pour the water into the sink.

7. Stand your bottle in the bowl. Fill the bowl with ice.

8. Add cold water to the ice. Hold the bottle straight.

9. Wait three minutes. Draw what you see:

10. The water changed the temperature of the air in the bottle.

Hot air takes up _____ space than cold air.

Circle one: more / less

 **Next Question**

Find two helium balloons. One is in a warm room. It is filled with hot air. One is in a cold room. It is filled with cold air. Which one rises higher?

 Notebook Reflection

Name three things that you can fill with air.

What's Inside a Pebble?

Name _____

What You Need:
- 10 pebbles
- magnifying glass
- large clear plastic jar
- water

What To Do:

1. Use a magnifying glass to look closely at one pebble.

2. Draw what you see.

3. Place all the pebbles in the plastic jar. Draw what you see.

4. Pour water over the pebbles. Draw what you see.

pebbles in jar	pebbles under water

5. What changed? What didn't?

 **Next Question**

Use a hammer to break apart the pebbles. What's inside?

 Notebook Reflection

Why do you think the pebbles were different under water?

How Can I Group Rocks?

Name _____

What You Need:
- lots of rocks
- magnifying glass
- water
- shallow bowl

What To Do:

1. Look at the rocks. Use a magnifying glass to look closely.

2. Put the rocks into two groups: small and big.

3. Draw the rocks in the two boxes:

small rocks	big rocks

4. Now put all the rocks into three groups: small, bigger, and biggest.

5. Draw the rocks in the three boxes:

small rocks	bigger rocks	biggest rocks

How Can I Group Rocks (cont.)

What To Do: (cont.)

6. Put the rocks in a bowl. Pour some water on them.

7. Put the wet rocks into groups of different colors.

8. Make a box for each color and draw the rocks that go in that box.

? Next Question

When the rocks dry out, are they still the same color? How could you put them in new color groups?

Notebook Reflection

What is another way to sort rocks into groups?

Astronomy

This chapter provides activities that address McREL Science Standard 3.

Student understands the composition and structure of the universe and the Earth's place in it.

Knows basic patterns of the Sun and Moon (e.g., the Sun appears every day and the Moon appears sometimes at night and sometimes during the day; the Sun and Moon appear to move from east to west across the sky; the Moon appears to change shape over the course of a month; the Sun's position in the sky changes through the seasons)	What Does the Solar System Look Like?, page 49 How Does the Moon Change?, page 50 How Do the Sun and Moon Move?, page 52 How Does the Sun Rise?, page 54
Knows that the stars are innumerable, unevenly dispersed, and of unequal brightness	Why Are Some Stars Brighter Than Others?, page 56

How to Teach Astronomy

Astronomy: It's a Big Subject

For many reasons, teaching about Earth in space is not easy. Children come to school with their own ideas about space, and some of those ideas are very difficult to dislodge.

They may believe, for example, that the Sun moves and Earth stands still. Given that the Sun apparently moves across the sky, this is understandable. Although the idea was questioned by Copernicus and later disproved by Galileo, the movement of the Sun was accepted science until the fifteenth century. This reflects our own observation, of course. Other commonly-held incorrect ideas include the theory that the Moon covers the Sun at night; that the shadow of Earth is what causes the apparent change in the shape of the Moon; and that the Sun is slightly further away from Earth in the winter (when in fact the opposite is true during winter in the northern hemisphere).

Three Important Concepts

Where Earth, Sun, and Moon are concerned, there are three important concepts to tackle. With these understood, the relationships of Earth, Sun, and Moon become clear.

1 Size

Earth, Sun, and Moon are all spherical—a function of the force of gravity, which pulls all matter toward the center of an object. Since the heavenly bodies are subject to their own force of gravity, they are all pulled towards their middles, and so tend to be ball-shaped. Very small objects in space don't have this large gravity force and so remain irregular in shape.

The heavenly bodies are subject to other gravity forces. The Sun's gravity keeps Earth and all the other planets in orbit. Earth's gravity keeps the Moon in orbit.

Because books often need to fit all three into a small picture, students have little idea of their relative sizes. You could fit a million Earths into the Sun. The differences are literally astronomical.

	Circumference	Diameter
Sun	4,370,880 km	1,392,000 km
Earth	40,076 km	12,756 km
Moon	10,915 km	3,476 km

2 Distance

If you model the Sun with a beach ball, Earth is about the size of a pea and the Moon the size of a peppercorn. Then the beach ball and pea would be placed 40 meters apart to approximate scale. In reality, Earth is about 152 million km from the Sun.

The Sun and the Moon appear to be the same size in the sky. The Sun is much further away, so although it is much bigger than the Moon, both look the same size. In the same way that you can cover a distant mountain with your thumbnail, so—rarely—the Moon covers the Sun, blotting it out completely. This event is called a solar eclipse.

3 Movement

The Sun is actually moving and spinning, together with the whole Solar System and the galaxy. For the sake of simplicity, let's imagine it is still. Earth orbits the Sun and spins as it does so. Both orbit and spin are counter-clockwise viewed from above. The orbit gives us our year; the spin gives us day and night.

How to Teach Astronomy *(cont.)*

Day and Night

Earth spins on its axis. Every 24 hours, it makes one complete rotation. It rotates counter-clockwise, seen from above. We call this complete turn a day. Part of Earth is always facing the Sun. This part is in daylight. Part will be facing away from the Sun. For this part of Earth, it is nighttime. As Earth spins, each part of Earth moves from light to dark and back to light again—from day to night, and back to day. From Earth, it looks as though the Sun is moving across the sky. However, it is Earth that is turning while the Sun stands still.

The Moon

The Moon is orbiting us. Since it always has its face turned towards us, the back of the Moon (incorrectly called the "dark" side) is constantly away from us. For this to happen, the Moon has to spin as well as orbit. Rotation and orbit are synchronized, so as it moves around Earth, the Moon turns to keep the same side facing Earth.

The Moon's orbit is not in the plane of the other planets. Since it bobs up and down, it can appear in many places in the sky (and during both day and night, though it is blotted out by the Sun's brightness as often as not).

The Moon is not a light source. It reflects the Sun's light. Because the Moon orbits around Earth through the month, it presents different sides to the Sun. When we on Earth can see all of the sunlit side, we call this a full Moon. When we can only see a little bit of the sunlit side, we call it a crescent, and so on.

The Seasons

Earth is going around the Sun. The time it takes to complete a full orbit—365 and a quarter days—we call a year.

Earth's axis is at a slight angle to the Sun: 23.5° to be exact. This angle stays the same as Earth orbits the Sun. Each pole spends some of the year leaning towards the Sun and in strong sunlight. This is summer in that hemisphere. It spends some of the year leaning away from the Sun, and then it will be winter there.

Planets in the Solar System

There are eight known planets orbiting the Sun. They are, in order from the Sun outwards:

- Mercury
- Venus
- Earth
- Mars
- Jupiter
- Saturn
- Uranus
- Neptune

Together, these planets make the Solar System. The planets vary greatly in size—and they aren't as close together as shown here!

How to Teach Astronomy *(cont.)*

Sizes and Distances

The planets vary greatly in size. Jupiter, the biggest, is 143,000 km across at the equator; Mercury, the smallest, less than 5,000 km across. If you model the planets using fruit, then Jupiter could be a watermelon and Mercury a blueberry, while Earth would be about the size of a strawberry.

The distances between the planets are enormous. If a house were your model of the Sun and you set off with your planet fruits, you would have to carry them away down the road to model the distances. The Mercury blueberry might not even be in the same town! Mercury orbits the Sun every 88 Earth days, but Neptune takes 165 Earth years to make a complete orbit.

It is even further to the nearest star (after our Sun). If Earth were a football, the next star would be on the other side of the planet!

Fascinating Fact

The Sun is a gigantic light source. Its surface is at a temperature of over 5,000° C. In the center, where nuclear reactions are turning hydrogen to helium, the temperature is 15 million° C. Although the Sun is around 150 million kilometers from us, its light can still harm your eyes if you look straight at it. Light from the Sun is reflected by the rocky Moon, which makes the Moon shine at night and gives us moonlight.

Fascinating Fact

Some parts of the Solar System are very hot—it is 465° C on Venus. Some are very cold—it is –220° C on Pluto.

How to Teach Astronomy *(cont.)*

Many Moons

Earth is not the only planet with a moon. Mars has two moons: Phobos and Deimos. Jupiter has at least 16 moons, including Io and Europa. Saturn has about 23 moons, Uranus has 15, and Neptune has 8.

Other Citizens of the Solar System

In addition to the planets and their moons, the Solar System also has a number of other bodies within the orbits of the planets. Some of these also orbit the Sun, but others are merely drifting or orbit the planets, instead.

Dwarf planets like Pluto and Ceres are rocky bodies that have enough gravity to pull themselves into a sphere. Unlike planets, however, they are not large enough to clear their orbital path, and share the path with other objects. Ceres orbits within the asteroid belt; Pluto's orbit crosses Neptune's.

Comets have an icy head and a tail of dust and gas. They don't always trail their tail behind them. In fact, because the tail is always pointed away from the Sun, the tail goes first through half its orbit.

Asteroids are pieces of rubble. There is a belt of asteroid rubble between Mars and Jupiter.

Meteors are stony objects, some as small as a grain of sand. When they burn up in Earth's atmosphere, we call them shooting stars. Meteorites are larger. Some crash through the atmosphere and hit Earth.

Who's Orbiting Who?

Galileo said Earth orbited the Sun. He was prosecuted by the Inquisition because people didn't believe him. They believed the evidence of their own eyes. They saw the Sun rise, climb into the sky, sink, set, and dip below the horizon. They believed they saw a moving Sun. However, the Sun doesn't move around Earth. Earth moves around the Sun. To us on the moving Earth, this looks exactly the same as a moving Sun. No wonder people were confused!

Hazel on the Train

Here's an example to help illustrate this sometimes confusing concept.

Hazel was sitting in a train with her mother. She looked out of the window on her left. She could see into another train. She looked out of the window on her right. She could see the station. There were people standing on the platform. She looked back to her left. The windows of the train next to her were moving slowly past her window.

"That train is leaving the station!" she said to her mum.

"No, dear," said her mother. "That train is standing still. WE are leaving the station!"

Hazel looked to her right. Sure enough, they were passing the people on the platform. Her train was moving.

Hazel's train is like Earth, and the other train is like the Sun. Hazel's train is moving, and the other train is standing still.

What Does the Solar System Look Like?

Name _____

What You Need:
- colored clay
- paper
- pencil
- a measuring tape
- scissors
- beach ball

What To Do:

1. Use the chart below to make clay balls to represent each planet.

Planet's Name	Diameter Across	Distance from the Sun
Sun	75 cm diameter ball	0 cm
Mercury	.25 cm	1.25 cm
Venus	.6 cm	2.5 cm
Earth	.6 cm	3.75 cm
Mars	.25 cm	6.25 cm
Jupiter	8 cm	10 cm
Saturn	6.25 cm	40 cm
Uranus	2.5 cm	75 cm
Neptune	2.5 cm	1.2 m

2. Use pieces of paper to label each planet as well as its distance from the edge of the Sun.

3. Arrange the planets in the correct order.

 Next Question

The planets orbit around the Sun. It takes Earth about 365 days to make one complete revolution (trip) around the Sun. Which planets would need fewer days to complete their revolutions? Why?

 Notebook Reflection

If you were to use objects the correct size to represent all of the planets, what could you use instead of clay? What would the new solar system model look like?

How Does the Moon Change?

Name _____

What You Need: • the Moon

What To Do:

1. On a clear day, go outside after dark. Can you find the Moon?

2. Circle the shape the Moon looks most like.

How Does the Moon Change? *(cont.)*

Name _____

What You Need:

3. Check the Moon once a week for four weeks. Draw it each week.

week 1	week 2

week 3	week 4

4. What do you notice?

_____

_____

_____

Next Question

Is the Moon in the same place each time you find it? Why do you think that is?

Notebook Reflection

Use words and pictures to describe how the Moon looks like it changes.

How Do the Sun and Moon Move?

Name _____

What You Need:
- two pieces of construction paper
- a marker
- a globe

What To Do:

1. Push all the desks and chairs to the wall.

2. Form a group of four.

3. Make two signs. Write SUN on one. Write MOON on one.

4. Pick a person to stand in the center holding the SUN sign.

5. Pick a person to hold the globe. He or she walks slowly around the SUN in a circle. In space, it takes Earth one year to go around the Sun. This means that it takes 365 days.

6. Pick a person to spin the globe. In space, it takes 24 hours for Earth to make one complete spin. What do we call 24 hours?

   _____

7. The last person takes the MOON sign and walks in a circle around the globe.

How Do the Sun and Moon Move? *(cont.)*

What To Do: *(cont.)*

8. Now you are moving like the Earth and Moon in space!
Draw a picture that shows how the Earth and Moon move.
Use arrows to show their motion.

 Next Question

What happens when the person holding the globe tilts the top toward the Sun? What happens when that person moves to the opposite side of the Sun?

Notebook Reflection

When a thing orbits, it goes around something else. A thing rotates when it spins. Make a chart with the Sun, Earth, and Moon. Under each write "orbits" if it moves around another object. Write "rotates" if it spins.

How Does the Sun Rise?

Name _____

What You Need:
- desk
- flashlight
- hand mirror
- sticker

What To Do:

1. Place the sticker on the front of your shirt. You are the Earth. The sticker acts like your home.

2. Turn on the flashlight. Set it on the desk. The flashlight acts like the Sun.

3. Turn off the lights. Pull the blinds.

4. Stand one foot away from the desk. Face the flashlight.

5. Draw the pattern the light makes on your shirt:

Your home is in the _____.

Fill in the blank: *light / darkness*

On the front of your shirt it is _____.

Fill in the blank: *day / night*

How Does the Sun Rise? *(cont.)*

What To Do: *(cont.)*

6. Turn slowly to the left. Stop when your back faces the light.

Your home is in the_____.

Fill in the blank: light / darkness

On the front of your shirt it is _____.

Fill in the blank: day / night

7. Pick up the mirror. It acts like the Moon. Light from the Sun bounces off the Moon. Move the mirror so that light hits the front of your shirt.

8. Draw the light from the flashlight and mirror. Use arrows to show that the light bounces off the mirror.

9. Turn to the left until you face the flashlight.

On the front of your shirt it is _____.

Fill in the blank: day / night

? Next Question

Have a friend hold the mirror. Stand still. Your friend will walk around you with the mirror pointing at you. What happens on the dark side of your shirt?

Notebook Reflection

Draw the Sun, the Moon and the Earth in your science notebook. Use a yellow and a black marker to show how the light reflects. Label one side of Earth "day" and the other "night."

Why Are Some Stars Brighter than Others?

Name _____

What You Need: • 2 flashlights with good batteries

What To Do:

1. Find two partners. Hand them flashlights.
2. Turn off the lights. Pull the blinds.
3. Have your partners stand side by side and turn on their flashlights.
4. Take 10 steps back from them.
5. Look quickly at each light. Which one is brighter?
   Circle one: left / right / they're the same
6. Tell the partner on your left to take 7 steps back.
7. Look quickly at each light. Which one is brighter?
   Circle one: left / right / they're the same
8. Draw what you see.

Why Are Some Stars Brighter Than Others? *(cont.)*

What To Do: *(cont.)*

9. Why do you think this happened?

_____

_____

10. Think of the night sky. Are some stars brighter than others?

_____

_____

11. Why do you think this happens?

_____

_____

12. Switch places with a partner. Each of you must have a turn looking at the lights.

? Next Question

Use white paper and tape to make a tube that fits over the end of the flashlight. Have the partner is farthest away hold the tube over the flashlight. Does that light look brighter?

Notebook Reflection

List some ideas why some stars are brighter than others. Think of as many as you can.

Heredity

This chapter provides activities that address McREL Science Standard 4.

Student understands the principles of heredity and related concepts.

Knows that many characteristics of plants and animals are inherited from its parents (e.g., eye color in human beings, fruit or flower color in plants), and other characteristics result from an individual's interactions with the environment (e.g., people's table manners, ability to ride a bicycle)	

How to Teach Heredity

Students are growing and changing, illustrating how we all change as we mature and age. They may well have had experiences with birth and death through family or their pets; they may be beginning to understand the cyclical nature of life.

Reproduction is the process of making young. Each species reproduces its own kind. People make people. Dogs make dogs. Trees make trees. Reproduction is needed for species to survive.

Asexual Reproduction

There are two forms of reproduction. In asexual reproduction, something can reproduce all by itself. It does not need a partner. One parent cell divides. It forms two new cells. The cells are identical to the parent cell. Bacteria cells reproduce asexually. Most plants have the ability to reproduce asexually, too.

Sexual Reproduction

Sexual reproduction involves the combining of genetic material from both parents to produce a new individual. It happens with both plants and animals. Sometimes the product of the process doesn't even look alive. Some students believe that hens' eggs and seeds are not alive, though in changed circumstances either may produce new life—though not, of course, "breakfast eggs" which are not fertilized.

Research has shown that for many students, new life is formed from components or parts—new human babies manufactured "in a mommy's tummy" from bits, and chicks assembled from kits of legs, wings, head, and body floating around inside the egg.

It's just not like that. All life begins as a single cell—usually the result of combining the cells of two different parents. But there can be reproduction without fertilization—asexual reproduction and even cloning.

Sexual reproduction has the great advantage that it mixes the characteristics of parent organisms and gives them a big stir. The resulting offspring has characteristics from both parents.

Making a Baby

When animals reproduce sexually, they make special sex cells, each containing half a complete set of DNA. Fertilization is the process that combines these two cells to make a new one. The new cell will have a complete set of DNA.

Because the male cells—the sperm—need water to swim in, many animals reproduce in water. Amphibians like toads and frogs need to return to the water to breed. Land animals have developed internal fertilization. The male puts the sperm inside the female's body. Then the new animal develops in a mini-pond—the egg—or inside the mother in the womb. The egg, or the mother's womb, provides a food supply for the developing animal. Eggs are laid and eventually hatch. Mammals are born when the young animal is pushed from the mother's body.

Do Plants Have Babies?

While many students can accept that animals reproduce sexually, very few believe that plants reproduce sexually, perhaps because they may equate sexual reproduction with copulation.

How Plants Reproduce

Most green plants have special structures called flowers. Flowers are the reproductive parts of the plant. Flowers are fine examples of biodiversity. There is a huge range of types, in many colors, patterns, and shapes. But they all have the same aim—the continuation of the species.

The geranium is a plant with soft, furry leaves. Often, the flowers are red or pink. You can make new plants from an old one. Carefully break off a side branch from the main stem by pulling it downwards. Press your cutting into a small pot of compost or soil. Water it regularly. It will grow roots and eventually become a plant exactly like its parent. You have created a clone!

Life follows a distinct cycle, with birth, growth, and reproductive phases—always ending in death. Understandably, animal metamorphosis—the spectacular life-cycle in which animals undergo huge changes, such as caterpillar to butterfly or tadpole to frog—catches the imagination. But most animals produce young that resemble the adult—even those that go through partial metamorphosis—a "nymph" stage.

Plant reproduction can be equally interesting, especially if—like many primary-aged students—you believe that seeds grow in packets at the gardening store!

Male and female plant cells must be brought together for seeds to form. This process is called pollination. The male stamens produce pollen in their anthers. The pollen is carried to another flower by the wind or by insects. When the pollen grain reaches the stigma of another flower, it grows a pollen tube down to the female ovule. The ovule is fertilized and forms a seed. The ovary becomes a fruit: the container of the seed.

Green plants carry flowers, whose sole purpose in life is to ensure that their ovum is fertilized by pollen from another plant, either wind-blown or delivered by insects. Flowering plants produce seeds which are carried away, ensuring that when the new plants grow, they do not compete with their parents. The seeds are commonly carried on (strawberry) or inside (apple) fruits. These fruits are often intended to be eaten–which is good news for us and for other animals. The seeds may be discarded, or they may pass through the eater to reach the ground and germinate. Seeds of other fruits—like the tufts of the dandelion—are carried on the wind.

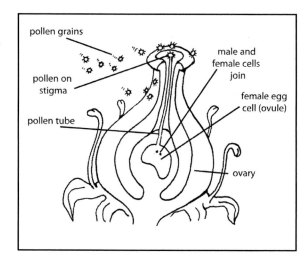

What Is a Chromosome?

How can we understand why humans are the way we are? We have to look at our cells. We must look at a material found in the center of our cells. This material is our chromosomes.

Chromosomes are found in each of our cells. We have 23 pairs of chromosomes. That means each cell has 46 in all. Chromosomes are made up of alleles. Each one has more than 2,000 alleles along its length. Alleles are instructions for cells.

How to Teach Heredity (cont.)

Because chromosomes come in pairs, alleles come in pairs, too. Each cell has two sets of instructions for everything. Two paired alleles work together to make a gene.

A zebra's genes give it stripes. A bird's genes give it wings. Our genes give us fingers and everything else that makes us human. Stripes, wings, and fingers are all traits. Those traits start in the cells. Each cell follows its gene's instructions on how to develop and work. All the cells work together to make stripes, wings, or fingers.

Remember how each cell has two sets of instructions for everything? A full set of chromosomes has 23 pairs. Each pair has one chromosome from the mother and one from the father. If the father were blonde and the mother were blonde, the chromosomes they gave the baby would have blonde alleles. Then the baby would be blonde.

Sometimes the mother and father do not have the same alleles. Then the baby gets chromosomes with different alleles on them. The father's chromosome may have the attached earlobe allele. The mother's chromosome may have the unattached earlobe allele. The baby's cells follow both sets of instructions at the same time. What kind of earlobes will the baby have?

Some alleles are dominant. Others are recessive. If a dominant allele is present, that trait will show up. So, if two dominant alleles are present, the dominant trait will show up. When one dominant and one recessive allele are present, the dominant allele will still show up. However, if two recessive alleles are present, the recessive trait will show up.

Alleles are passed down over generations. A recessive allele can "hide" behind dominant alleles for many generations before popping up and surprising the whole family with blue eyes or red hair.

How Did I Get My Eye Color?

Name _____

What You Need:
- family pictures (optional)
- paper
- pencil

What To Do:

1. Make a family tree showing your family. (Do not include the family pets!)

2. Fill in the eye color for each family member.

3. Eye color is based upon genetics (features or traits that you inherit from your parents, grandparents, great-grandparents, etc.). The order of eye color strength, from dominant (strongest) to most recessive (weakest) is brown, green, and blue.

 Next Question

Extend your family tree to include the eye color of grandparents, great-grandparents, and cousins. What do you notice about your family's eye color?

Notebook Reflection

If this same chart were made to reflect your family's (natural) hair color, what would be the dominant hair color? What would the recessive hair color be?

How Are Babies Like Their Parents?

Name _____

What You Need:
- sheet of paper
- crayons
- card with the name of an animal

What To Do:

1. Get in a group of three.

2. Fold your paper in half top to bottom.

3. Now fold the paper in half again.

4. Hold the paper like it is a book. Open the book. Number each page in the upper corner. Start with number 2. Write 3 on the other page.

5. On the back of the book, write 4. On the front write 1.

6. Think of an animal.

7. Draw the animal on page 2 of your book.

8. On page 3, draw a picture of the baby that animal would have.

9. Fold the book so page 2 isn't showing. When the teacher tells you, pass your book to your right.

10. Look at page three of your new book. Imagine that baby animal grown up. Draw the grown-up animal on page 4.

11. Fold the book so page 4 isn't showing. Pass the book to the right when the teacher tells you to.

12. Look at the animal on page 4. On page 1, draw the baby that animal would have.

What To Do: *(cont.)*

13. Pass the book to the right. Look at pages 4 and 1. Are those animals similar to the animals you drew? List three ways they are like your animals and three ways they are different.

_____

_____

_____

_____

_____

_____

? Next Question

As some babies grew up, they got traits that helped them live longer. They had more babies than the others. Look at the pictures in your book. Did either of the baby animals change in a way that helped them find more food or stay alive?

Notebook Reflection

Draw a family of five dogs. The mother is a Dalmatian and the father is a Laborador Retriever. They have three puppies. Will the puppies all look alike? Do they look just like their parents?

How Are Seeds Different?

Name _____

What You Need: • lots of different seeds

• jar with lid

What To Do:

1. Put all the seeds in a jar.

2. Choose a seed. Take it out and look at it carefully.

3. Draw a picture of your seed below.

4. Put the seed back in the jar. Shake the seeds around.

5. Try to find your seed again. How do you know it's the same seed?

_____

_____

 Next Question

Do the activity again. Compare the new drawing with the old one. What's different? What's the same?

Notebook Reflection

Describe how you found your seed the second time. What worked? What didn't?

What Are Fingerprints?

Name _____

What You Need: • soft pencil   • paper
                   • clear tape

What To Do:

1. Look closely at the tips of your fingers. Describe the patterns you can see.

   _____

   _____

   _____

2. Rub your pencil onto the paper.

3. Rub your fingertip in the pencil.

4. Press your fingers into the spaces on the next page.

5. Cover your fingerprints with clear tape so they don't smudge.

 **What To Do:** *(cont.)*

Left Hand

Right Hand

 **Next Question**

On a separate piece of paper, leave a few fingerprints. Label the page Evidence. Mix up the evidence pages with other students. Try to match the evidence pages to the first fingerprint pages.

 Notebook Reflection

Look carefully at your fingerprints. Use words to describe what you see. Are there patterns? Compare one print to another. What is the same? What is different?

Biology

This chapter provides activities that address McREL Science Standard 5.

Student understands the structure and function of cells and organisms.

How to Teach Biology

Cell Theory

The foundation of modern biology is cell theory. Cell theory has three parts:

- All living things are made of cells.
- Cells are the smallest part of living things that are themselves alive.
- All cells come from other cells.

Cells are microscopic clumps of chemicals bound by membranes. Inside the cell, complex organic chemicals receive materials from outside of the cell, break those materials apart to release energy and nutrients, and then use that energy and nutrients to make new materials that the cell needs. The chemicals receive "instructions" from the cell's DNA—itself an incredible complex organic chemical. In fact, the instructions are passed along from the DNA to the rest of the cell through chemical reactions.

The vast majority of living things on planet Earth, both in number and by biomass, are organisms made up of one cell. The rest of the living world—and the part that we're most familiar with—consists of organisms made of more than one cell: plants, animals, and the occasional fungus.

Animals

Animals are multicellular heterotrophs. They are composed of more than one cell (multicellular), and they eat other organisms to survive (heterotroph).

The hardest part of any animal's life is staying alive! To do this animals need to:

- eat
- keep warm
- evade hunters

Food

Animals need food for energy. They release that energy by a cellular process called respiration. (It mustn't be forgotten that plants respire, too; they do not produce food as a selfless activity to support the animal kingdom.) Respiration and the release of energy from food require oxygen. Animals are unable to store oxygen. It is the need to regularly renew oxygen stores that leads them to breathe in different ways—through breathing tubes (insects); through gills (fish and young amphibians); through their skin and the lining of their mouths (frogs); or with lungs (reptiles, birds, and mammals).

This process releases the energy needed for life. Animals need to maintain this process to survive. This makes the finding and ingesting of food an imperative for every animal on Earth.

Heat

Living things function because of chemical reactions in their bodies. These chemical reactions run faster and more efficiently in warmer conditions. Their body temperature varies with their environment. Cold-blooded animals become less active in cold conditions—or may boost their body temperature by basking in the sun.

Mammals and birds maintain their body temperature as if they had an internal thermostat. Since these animals need to maintain these temperatures, they are affected by seasonal change. They may stay active throughout the cold conditions, evade them by going somewhere warmer (migration), or become inactive for weeks at a time (hibernation).

Run, Hide... or Fight Back.

Animals have a variety of ways of evading their predators. They might be able to outrun them—as in the case of the hare escaping the fox. But if they can't, then what other tricks do they have up their sleeves? One option is camouflage, by which the animal changes in some way to match its surroundings. Examples include the changing color of the chameleon and the stick insect who looks just like the twig she is sitting on.

Some animals need have no fear of enemies because they are so unpleasant-tasting, or poisonous, that they can be vividly-colored, advertising their unpleasantness. A bright red ladybird presumably tastes disgusting to a bird. Many spiders and scorpions have a deadly bite or sting, and some tarantulas are happy to stand back and fire irritating hairs at their enemies.

Perceiving the World

Animals need sense organs to find their way around. Putting the sense organs at the front or top of the body makes them more useful. If the animal is a secondary consumer—a predator or carnivore—the sense organs are likely to be forward-facing, enabling it to see its prey and to catch it efficiently. If the animal is a primary consumer, or herbivore, then its sense organs are likely to survey the surroundings more generally. It needs to be aware of predators and danger. Cats have eyes on the front of their heads; mice have them on the side. Cats have excellent, stereoscopic forward vision to catch mice; mice have good all-around vision to spot and avoid cats.

Fascinating Facts

What Is a Life-Cycle?

The process of birth, growth, reproduction, aging, and death is the animal's life-cycle.

Animals' longest-known life span

adult mayfly	3 days
mouse	3 years
guppy	5 years
large beetles	5–10 years
swallow	9 years
coyote	15 years
giant spider	20 years
toad	36 years
lobster	50 years
crocodile	60 years
sea anemone	70 years
elephant	77 years
blue whale	80 years
golden eagle	80 years
sturgeon	100 years
tortoise	100–150 years
human	113 years

Plants

Plants are multicellular autotrophs. They are composed of more than one cell (multicellular), and they produce their own food (autotroph).

Plants Are Alive!

Yes, plants are alive, too! Piaget first identified the stages that students move through in their understanding of "the life concept." His research suggests that at a young age, movement is equated with life. Things that appear to move by themselves—including rivers and the Sun—are deemed alive.

If that type of confusion seems improbable, consider the apple you are about to eat for your lunch. You may have difficulty in believing that it is alive—not the plant from which it came, but the apple itself. It respires using its own food source, excretes waste gases, and could reproduce, given the right conditions for its seeds. No wonder that, while all 8- to 11-year-olds appear to agree that plants grow, only 69 percent of them regard plants as living.

Animals clearly show the seven life processes, but plants—which may look dead at some times of the year—show them all, too.

1. Nutrition: Green plants can make their own food, but they need that food to grow and live.

2. Growth: Plants grow, sometimes very slowly. But a new seedling grows a lot faster than a human baby!

3. Reproduction: Plants can produce seeds or spores. Some plants reproduce by growing new plants from special stems or roots.

4. Respiration: Plants need oxygen to live, and they produce carbon dioxide. Fortunately for us, they produce a lot of oxygen, too!

5. Sensitivity: Plants are sensitive to their surroundings. Climbing bean plants sense a stick, and twine around it.

6. Excretion: Plants produce waste products—a little carbon dioxide and a lot of oxygen.

7. Movement: Plants move. Some move quite fast, like mimosa, the sensitive plant that closes its leaves when you touch it. Others move more slowly, like the dandelions that open for the Sun, and close at night.

Making Their Own Food

Green plants are the only living things able to make their own food. They combine water with carbon dioxide from the air and chlorophyll from the leaves to produce glucose (a type of sugar). This process needs light energy, usually from the Sun, and is called photosynthesis. Plants also need to absorb tiny quantities of mineral salts and other nutrients from the soil and we confuse this process by calling it "feeding" the plant. Plants don't feed—they are food producers and the first step in most food chains.

Don't forget that plants also respire, just like us. They don't breathe by mechanically drawing air into and expelling it from the body, but they use oxygen in their cells in the process that releases energy from stored foods. At night, they respire but do not photosynthesize. During the day, they are doing both. Fortunately for life on Earth, the amounts of oxygen plants use are exceeded by the amounts they produce.

How to Teach Biology *(cont.)*

Take a deep breath; here we go. To start with, photosynthesis takes place in two stages. In the first, sunlight is used to split water into oxygen and hydrogen. This depends upon the ability of a green pigment in plants called chlorophyll to split water molecules. The oxygen is now a waste product—which is a good thing for those of us who favor breathing.

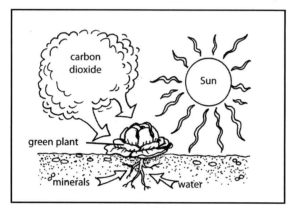

Next, a reaction takes place which doesn't need light. It takes place in a billionth of a second. The hydrogen (actually split into bits by now) is used to convert carbon dioxide into carbohydrates—basic building blocks for sugars, starch, and a wide range of materials. One of these is cellulose, the material that plant cell walls are made from. As a result, the plant has food for activity and material for growth, both of which we can exploit by eating a cucumber sandwich.

Why Are Plants That Shape?

To make their food by photosynthesis, plants need to catch the light of the Sun. Their whole structure is aimed at collecting and using as much sunlight as possible.

They have a branching root system that can grip the soil. There is as much tree below the ground as above it (the roots of a tree are roughly the same size and extent as its canopy). They have a strong stem (sometimes a trunk) that can hold the leaves up high—and above the leaves of competitors—and a mathematically—precise leaf pattern.

If you want to see the effectiveness of the leaf pattern, stand under a tree on a sunny day. The leaves are laid out to ensure that even the lower ones make use of the light missed by those above them. The result is nearly complete coverage.

Fungi Are NOT Plants!

Fungi are either saprotrophs or parasites. Saprotrophs eat non-living matter. Parasites get their energy and nutrients from a host organism without killing it first. Fungi may be multicellular, in the case of mushrooms, or unicellular, in the case of yeast.

Fungi are not green—they cannot make their own food like plants. They produce spores, not seeds. Their structure can spread for miles under the ground.

Microorganisms

Most single-celled or unicellular organisms are presently grouped into three kingdoms: protoctista, bacteria, and archaea. However, this is a temporary classification solution at best. These three kingdoms represent more diversity of life than all the other kingdoms combined.

Students call microorganisms "bugs" or "germs." These names include small invertebrates, bacteria, and viruses. The names are associated with dirt, death, and disease. Students may think of microorganisms as things that walk about inside us, eating, breeding, and making us ill. Given the opportunity, they would probably exterminate all microorganisms, thus inadvertently bringing the world to a speedy end!

Few students are aware of the beneficial effects of microorganisms and have little idea of their importance in decay and recycling. They may not understand that we live surrounded by microorganisms of all sorts, and that we are dependent on them for our health and well-being.

It's difficult to teach about microorganisms because you're teaching about something that is invisible to the naked eye. It's very hard to envision a microscopic world of the size and complexity that exists. It is harder still to give students actual experiences of that world.

In promoting the benefits of microorganisms, point out that they are essential to making leavened bread, cheese, yogurt, vinegar, and many protein meat substitutes. They are essential to the production of many medicines and the breakdown of sewage.

Fascinating Facts

Algae

The term "algae" can mean any number of different organisms that have little to no relation to each other and very little in common. Everything from seaweed to cyanobacteria has been counted as an algae at one time or another, to the point that the term itself is problematic at best.

Mini-Beasts

Some of the most accessible animals available to students are "mini-beasts"—insects, pillbugs, centipedes, even earthworms. These fascinating creatures can give students an up-close look at the basic needs and structure of animal life. These animals do not fall into a neat category. They are not all insects, but include arachnids, annelids, and even crustaceans in the case of the pillbug. This text refers to these scientific gold mines as "mini-beasts" and includes a number of labs investigating their small and educational world.

What Do Mini-Beasts Eat?

Name _____

What You Need:
- mini-beasts
- leaves
- vegetables
- flowers
- 4 trays
- 4 sheets of plastic

What To Do:

1. Spread the leaves, vegetables, and flowers evenly over the four trays.

2. Gently place three or four mini-beasts on each tray. Each tray should only have one kind of mini-beast.

3. Cover the trays with plastic. Poke small holes in the plastic so the mini-beasts can breathe.

4. Look at each tray every day for four days. Record what you see.

Tray #1	Tray #2	Tray #3	Tray #4
Type of Mini-Beast:	Type of Mini-Beast:	Type of Mini-Beast:	Type of Mini-Beast:
Favorite Food:	Favorite Food:	Favorite Food:	Favorite Food:
Least Favorite Food:	Least Favorite Food:	Least Favorite Food:	Least Favorite Food:

 **Next Question**

Use your school library or the Internet to research what mini-beasts eat.

 Notebook Reflection

Imagine you were the size of a mini-beast. Describe why different mini-beasts eat different foods.

What Is Mold?

Name _____

What You Need:
- sealable plastic bags
- fruit
- bread
- cotton balls
- water
- permanent marker

What To Do:

1. Use the marker to put your name on the bag.

2. Put a piece of fruit, some bread, and a damp cotton ball in the plastic bag. Seal it up.

3. Find a place in the classroom to put your bag where it will not be disturbed. Use the marker to write on the bag where you left it.

I left my bag here: _____

4. Leave the bags closed for two weeks. Check each day for changes. Draw what you see.

What Is Mold? *(cont.)*

What To Do: *(cont.)*

5. At the end of the two weeks, compare your bag with other students'. Draw two other bags below:

6. Where was the bag that grew the most mold?_____

Where was the bag that grew the least?_____

? Next Question	**Notebook Reflection**
Use a magnifying glass to look at the mold close-up. Draw what you see.	*Why do you think different bags grew different amounts of mold?*

What Is Inside Leaves?

Name _____

What You Need:
- large plastic container
- small plastic container
- small stone
- plastic sheeting
- string
- leaves
- magnifying glass

What To Do:

1. Gather enough leaves to half fill the large container.

2. Place the small container inside the large one. Arrange the leaves around the small container.

3. Cover the top with plastic. Secure it with string.

4. Make a dish shape in the top of the plastic over the small container. Place the stone on top to keep the shape.

5. Place the container outside in the sun for five days.

6. After five days, carefully remove the plastic. Observe the water that has gathered in the small container. Describe what you see. _____

_____

7. Use the magnifying glass to measure the volume of water in the small container. Volume: _____

 **Next Question**

Compare your results to the volumes of water other students gathered. Why might there be differences?

 Notebook Reflection

Where do you think the water came from? How do you think it got in the small container?

What Do Plants Need?

Name _____

What You Need:
- 3 clear plastic containers
- batting
- dry wheat seeds
- cold boiled water
- cooking oil
- soaked wheat seeds

What To Do:

1. Label the containers "Test 1," "Test 2," and "Test 3."
2. Place dry batting in the Test 1 container. Put dry wheat seeds on top of the batting. Do not water it.
3. Place dry wheat seeds in the Test 2 container.
4. Cover the wheat seeds with cold boiled water.
5. Pour cooking oil onto the water until a film forms on top.
6. Place the soaked seeds on damp batting in the Test 3 container. Keep the batting damp throughout the test.
7. Put the three containers in a warm, sunny place.
8. Predict what will happen to the seeds in each container.

container	prediction	week one	week two	week three
Test 1				
Test 2				
Test 3				

 Next Question

Perform the experiment with different seeds, such as beans or flowers. Do you get different results? Why?

 Notebook Reflection

Use words and pictures to explain why the seeds grew differently in different conditions.

How Do Mini-Beasts Live?

Name _____

What You Need:
- mini-beasts
- tweezers
- clear plastic sheet
- ruler
- trays
- water
- sand
- rocks
- flashlight

What To Do:

1. Use tweezers to carefully put one mini-beast on the clear plastic. Watch it from beneath. Write three words to describe how your mini-beast moves.

_____

_____

_____

2. Can the mini-beast move up a steep slope? Tip the tray and watch. Record what you see.

_____

_____

_____

3. Move the mini-beast to a piece of paper. Follow behind its path with a pencil for one minute.

4. Measure the line. How far did your mini-beast travel in one minute?

_____

_____

How Do Mini-Beasts Live? *(cont.)*

What To Do: *(cont.)*

5. Use rocks, water, and sand to make a landscape on the tray. Move your mini-beast to the landscape. Watch what it does.

6. What does the mini-beast do when it meets water?

_____

_____

_____

7. What does the mini-beast do when it meets a big rock?

_____

_____

_____

8. What does the mini-beast do when you shine the flashlight on it?

_____

_____

_____

How Do Mini-Beasts Live? *(cont.)*

What To Do: *(cont.)*

9. Draw your landscape and your mini-beast. Write a few sentences about what you learned.

How Are Plants Different?

Name _____

What You Need: • plastic hoop

What To Do:

1. Take the plastic hoop to an area with lots of plants.

2. Choose a spot that is similar to the rest of the area. Place your hoop flat on the grass.

3. Look closely at the plants inside your hoop. Draw or describe each plant. Give it a name.

How Are Plants Different? *(cont.)*

What To Do: *(cont.)*

4. Count the number of each different plant inside the hoop. Write the number of each plant next to its drawing.

5. Move your hoop to another place. Repeat steps #3 and #4.

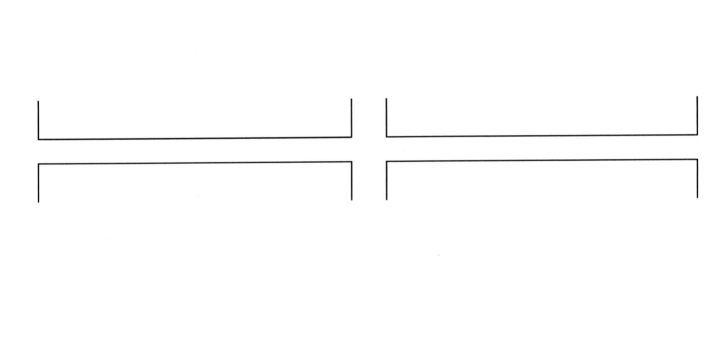

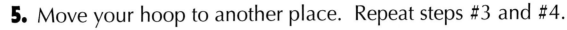

Next Question

Compare your results with the rest of the class. Did you choose the same plants as others? How do you know?

Notebook Reflection

How were the two places similar? How were they different?

How Do Feet Match Homes?

Name _____

What You Need: • many pictures of birds

What To Do:

1. Look at the pictures of birds. Look at their feet. Sort the birds according to their feet in the chart below.

2. Look at the pictures again. Look at the places they live. Write in the kind of habitat that each bird lives in next to the bird's name.

Type of Feet	Names of Birds	Habitat
Long toes		
Small toes		
Hooked toes		
Webbed toes		

 **Next Question**

Make a collage of bird pictures. Focus on their feet and their habitats.

 Notebook Reflection

How do birds' feet match their habitats?

How Do Beaks Match Breakfast?

Name _____

What You Need:
- colored thin cards
- scissors
- glue
- references for about 12 birds

What To Do:

1. Work in a group of four. Take turns picking birds.

2. Draw the bird's beak in a top space on the next page. Write the name of the bird above it. You can practice in the space below.

3. Draw the kind of food that the bird eats in the box below its beak. Write the name of the food below it.

4. Pick another bird that no one else has done. Repeat steps #2 and #3 for your new bird. Do three birds this way.

How Do Beaks Match Breakfast? *(cont.)*

What To Do: *(cont.)*

5. Cut out the six pictures below and glue them to the cards. Make sure each card has a bird's beak on one side and the food it eats on the other.

6. Shuffle the cards together. Take turns holding up a card. Show one side to another student in your group. Can they guess the other side? Play this game until you go through all the cards two or three times.

 **Next Question**

What other animals have body parts that match what they eat?

 Notebook Reflection

How do beaks match breakfast?

What Is in My Square Meter?

What You Need:
- mini-beasts
- magnifying glass
- square meter

What To Do:

1. Take your square meter outside and place it on the ground somewhere. Set it on grass, or in a garden, or on dirt.

2. Use a magnifying glass to examine four different mini-beasts you find inside your square meter.

3. Draw your mini-beasts. Label their features.

? Next Question

Find the names of your mini-beasts and other information about them.

Notebook Reflection

How were your mini-beasts similar? How were they different?

How Do Seeds Work?

Name _____

What You Need:
- broad bean seed soaked overnight
- variety of other seeds

What To Do:

1. Carefully open the broad bean seed. Ask your teacher to cut it open if needed.

2. Examine the embryo.

3. Draw and label the parts of the embryo that look like a plant.

#50163—Science Labs: Standards-Based Investigations—K–2

What To Do: *(cont.)*

4. Examine the different seeds. Draw them.

5. Each type of seed has a different cover for the embryo. Suggest reasons why different plant seeds need different covers.

_____

_____

_____

 Next Question

Examine the different seeds. Think about how the seeds travel. How do the seed shapes help?

 Notebook Reflection

Imagine you are the plant embryo inside the seed. Draw or write about how that would feel.

Ecology

This chapter provides activities that address McREL Science Standard 6.

Student understands relationships among organisms and their physical environment.

Knows that plants and animals need certain resources for energy and growth (e.g., food, water, light, air)	Do Plants Need Sunshine?, page 97 How Much Can I Breathe?, page 99 How Far Can Plants Reach?, page 101 What do I Need?, see Teacher CD
Knows that living things are found almost everywhere in the world and that distinct environments support the life of different types of plants and animals	What is in my Square Meter Now?, page 103

How to Teach Ecology

It's easy to forget that the natural world underpins our very lives, especially if you live in an urban environment. When your food comes prepackaged, and the only plants you see are in parks and flower shops, you can overlook the close relationship we all have with the natural world. Perhaps that's why we choose to take breaks in the countryside and succumb to the attraction of gardening. These activities bring us closer to the plants and animals we depend on.

Do Animals Need Plants?

We certainly do! Without plants, animals, including us humans, wouldn't survive—and I don't mean just because we eat them!

If we were dependent on the stored oxygen in the atmosphere for breathing, life on Earth would be finite. When the last of the oxygen had been used up (or actually, long before), most life on Earth would end. Even if we were to stop being so wasteful with the stuff—burning it or pumping it through our forms of transport—it would not last forever. It has to be renewed. Fortunately for us, green plants and algae are very good at that. All our oxygen is recycled again and again.

We would die long before the oxygen ran out, though. The reason for that is that the waste gas we breathe out—carbon dioxide—is poisonous in large quantities, and a buildup in the atmosphere would kill us. Fortunately, plants have a use for carbon dioxide. They recycle that too, using it to make food for themselves (and often, for animals) and produce oxygen!

This handy cycle ensures that life on Earth can continue indefinitely. True, plants need oxygen too, and yes, they produce some carbon dioxide, but this is far outweighed by the amount of oxygen they produce.

Plants give us more than just oxygen! We don't need plants just for gases. We can eat them (or we eat the animals that eat plants), and we use plant products for clothes, shelter, furniture, and medicines.

Without plants there would be no animal life on Earth. We need them. It is this complex relationship between plants and animals that makes their study so interesting.

It is the breakdown of this relationship, by pollution and the wholesale destruction of the rainforests, that threatens us and all other living things.

Do Plants Need Animals?

You wouldn't think so, would you? Everything they need is right there where they are growing. They have carbon dioxide from the air, water from the rain, and a pinch of mineral salts from the soil. Combining all these produces a living growing thing.

Do animals do anything for plants? Well yes, they do. They produce a large part of the carbon dioxide needed for plants to photosynthesize and live.

Just as important, animals provide a useful delivery system for living things that are literally rooted to the spot. If you have some dusty, yellow pollen that you are wanting to get to that plant over there, then what better way than hitching a lift on a furry insect traveling from flower to flower? Usefully, the honeybee has very casual standards of personal hygiene—and no clothes to brush. So it will fly off with pollen on its coat. Indeed, plants can even afford to sacrifice a bit as bee food—hence

the pollen sacs on the bee's legs. Plants provide a few encouragements—sweet nectar, bright colors, and even markings (bee lines) that help with a safe landing.

Bees, flies, other insects, some birds, and other animals offer this helpful service—and it doesn't stop there. When the pollen has been delivered, the egg has been fertilized, and the seeds have formed, they need distributing, too. Animals also provide a convenient—if erratic—delivery service for seeds.

The outsides of animals—the fur of mammals and the feathers of birds—provide a convenient hanging place for hooked burrs and sticky seeds. The insides happily accept tasty fruits and, if the seeds are resistant to digestion (with a hard coat), they will pass through the eater and be deposited somewhere far away, together with some waste matter rich in organic material (otherwise known as manure).

Many seeds are transported like this. Even the huge stones of the avocado tree are carried away by the birds that eat the fruit—though it is probably just as well that they don't pass right through the bird but are regurgitated. Otherwise the resplendent quetzal bird might be famed for its constipation!

It's as if the fruits of many seeds had a sign hanging on them saying, "Eat me." Their color, taste, and smell are all inviting, and it doesn't take long before an animal accepts their invitation. And if they don't? The fruit falls to the ground with its precious packet of seeds and may germinate anyway. But, without the animals—especially the birds—that feast on their fruits and carelessly drop their seeds from the skies, a lot of plants would be rooted to the spot in every sense.

The Biosphere

Earth is packed with living things. Every plant and animal lives in an environment on Earth. One more name for this environment is the "biosphere." The biosphere is the part of our Earth that supports life—the land, the water, and the lower atmosphere.

A Habitat

A plant's habitat is its address—the place where it lives. An animal's habitat is its address, too. Because most animals move around, an animal's habitat is wider and bigger. A cave, a woodland, a pond, or a forest floor are all habitats. So are canals, gardens, and playgrounds.

Habitats are places that provide a source of raw materials for growth and activity; a source of energy, either from the sun or from the plants that harness the sun's energy; shelter from changing conditions, from weather and from predators; and a place to dump the products of living.

An Environment

We use the word "environment" to describe our surroundings on Earth. Our environment is everything that affects us—the place where we live, our home and school, our weather, our food, water, and the air we breathe, the plants and animals we affect and that affect us, the special animals we call our friends and family—and also the strangers whose work and behavior affect us.

The Ecosystem

The plants and animals in a habitat are linked through food chains and webs. The animals may live by eating plants found in their habitat or by eating other animals that in turn eat the plants. This link between plants and animals and their habitat is called an ecosystem.

Lions eat gazelles that eat the green plants found on the African plains. They are in the same ecosystem. Gazelles don't eat seaweed, and lions don't eat penguins. They are not found in their habitat and so are not a part of their ecosystem.

Energetic Ecosystems

Ecosystems are about energy flow. Forget any romantic view of nature. Think of the plants and animals as links in this flow of energy. The first link in this chain is the green plant kingdom. Plants capture the sun's energy through a process called photosynthesis, whereby they make their own food. This energy is passed on to animals who eat the plants (herbivores) and then to meat-eating animals that eat the herbivores (carnivores). At any stage, nutrients are returned to the soil through the decomposition of waste—excrement and dead bodies—and the cycle is complete. So even the soil and the physical surroundings are part of the pattern.

This is not an efficient process—each link in the chain needs to keep some energy for itself. The plants need to live and grow. So do the animals. In addition, creatures like us need to stay warm—an expensive business in terms of energy. We can waste a lot of this energy as heat loss, too.

The whole thing is pretty fragile. The removal of just one species can unravel the ecosystem with terrifying speed. That's why environmental protesters can get so hot under the collar. Take, for example, the spread of myxomatosis among rabbits. This disease was welcomed by farmers when it began to wipe out these cuddly pests. But the decimation of the rabbit population was catastrophic for foxes, who began to look for food elsewhere, wandering suburban streets in search of full trash cans. At the other end of the scale, wild plant populations exploded, uncropped by rabbits. Suppose the fox population had been wiped out instead. The result would have been an explosion of rabbit numbers (remember, they would breed like rabbits!) and the green plants would be grazed to extinction. And then the starving rabbits would begin to die....

Food Chains

Why don't lions eat oranges?

Because they can't peel them, silly!

There are food chains in every habitat that ensure that organisms survive. You can see these food chains as a sort of energy flow and, ultimately, all that energy begins with the sun. It is the sun's energy that plants convert to their own structures, and hence to food. Green plants are the first link in most food chains.

After green plants, the next link is the plant-eaters. Finally, predators live off plant-eaters and also off each other. Food chains show how plants are eaten by plant-eaters, and plant-eaters are eaten by meat-eaters.

Of course, it's never quite as simple as that. Food chains with the direct line of the grass—zebra—lion type don't show the whole picture. Grass is eaten by more than just zebras; zebras eat more than just grass and are themselves eaten by more than just lions. And the lions eat more than just zebras.

How to Teach Ecology *(cont.)*

Food Webs

It is easier to understand this in terms of food webs. Aphids live off plants and ladybirds live off aphids. But the ladybird could meet any number of fates from insect-eating birds, who might themselves take a fancy to a juicy aphid….

A food web shows the animals that might live on or around a tree for example. In every food web, there are many different food chains. The food web in a woodland, for example, might involve some plant-eating consumers like grasshoppers and mice. A secondary consumer like a frog might not tackle a mouse but will make a meal of a grasshopper. Snakes are partial to frogs, but not averse to a mouse or a grasshopper, either. Hawks will eat a snake—or jump that link and go straight for a mouse.

Fascinating Fact

Not all food chains start with a green plant. There are deep-sea life forms that can harness chemical energy. These bacteria live in total darkness near the hydrothermal vents of the Pacific Ocean, in very high temperatures. Deep-sea animals eat the bacteria as other animals eat plants.

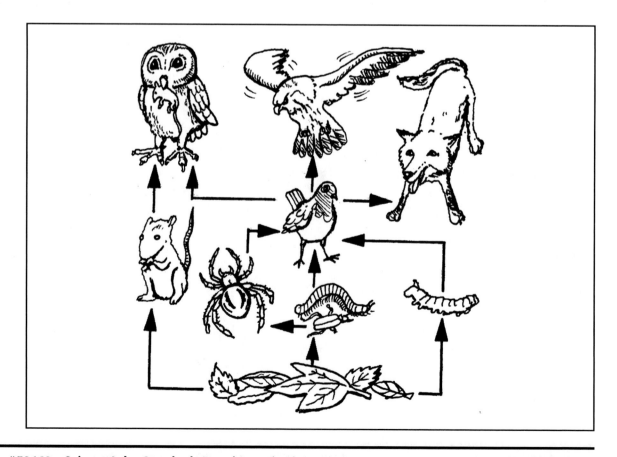

How to Teach Ecology *(cont.)*

Just Another Bypass

Of course the biggest ecosystem destroyer has two legs—and giant earthmovers and an unlimited supply of concrete. When a new road is pushed through a habitat, it rattles not just the plants and animals living there, but others that depend upon them. Well-meaning conservationists have attempted to save habitats by moving them—rolling up a meadow to make room for a supermarket, for example. But other factors—the soil, the exposure, the microclimate—are different, and these projects are seldom successful. It's not just the plants and animals that matter. It's every aspect of the ecosystem. The more we learn about the environment, the more we discover how closely everything is interlinked.

Changing Habitats

Habitats change naturally. They may change daily, when the sun comes up and goes down, or the tide goes in and out. They may change with the seasons, as it turns first cold and then warm again. They may change completely over short periods of time: after an earthquake, a flood, or a volcanic eruption. They may change completely over a longer period of time, as a river changes course or rocks wear away. Ponds dry up, trees die and are replaced by new young trees, and grass withers in a hot summer.

Habitats are also changed by outside influences. Faced with yet another grazed knee, the principal of a primary school decided that the uneven paving slabs would have to go. A smooth layer of asphalt was the answer: no breaks, no gaps, no edges to trip over. The job was quickly done; but a small habitat was destroyed.

The small plants had had a grip on the thin soil between the slabs; ants had nested in the soft bedding sand; worms, beetles, and other small invertebrates lived under and between the stones. Birds were occasional visitors: the thrush that had found both snails and a handy anvil and the woodpecker that had feasted on ants when the tree insects were few. With the birds gone, the neighborhood cat no longer lurked with a view to catching a bird.

We can't help environmental change, but we can be sensitive to the rolling effects of our actions. On a much larger scale, desertification is the process that renders fertile land arid and dead. Around the world, a hundred square kilometers are lost to desert every day. In Africa, a series of droughts has enlarged the Sahara southwards. These droughts may be linked to world climate change. But heavy grazing and deeper wells have disturbed the fertile Sahel region, so that the Sahara is growing at around 5 km a year.

So, habitats are always changing. Most plants and animals can adapt to small changes in their habitat. But some cannot. Most animals can move when the habitat changes and find somewhere else to live. Plants cannot. Animals may survive seasonal change by migrating or by hibernating. Big changes to a habitat can destroy populations of animals and plants. Some of those big changes are made by people.

Extinction

Plants and animals that cannot adapt to changed conditions die out. And because humans have been responsible for more environmental change than any other factor, humans have been responsible for a great many extinctions.

How to Teach Ecology *(cont.)*

More animals have become extinct in the past 300 years than in all the years before because of humans. We have changed habitats by farming, clearing trees, and building roads and houses. Animals like the dodo, the Tasmanian wolf, and the Balinese tiger have died out.

We Can't Stop Change

Some of the most major changes are the result of the human factor. By our use of land, we can change habitats and affect the lives of plants and animals. Our changes may be damaging—green field site development—or for the better—the landscaping of old industrial sites. We are learning to protect environments, recognizing the delicacy of environmental balance and the vulnerability of the natural world.

This may go against your lifestyle. You may be an inner-city dweller who never sees a blade of grass. But you are as dependent on the environment as anybody. And remember—nowhere is without life. You just need to get out more and look around you!

We are rightly concerned about environmental change—and especially environmental damage. But we would be wrong to think that habitats are unchanging. Every habitat is changing, even without human intervention. Animals and plants unable to survive these changes—annual, seasonal, or daily—will soon be extinct.

Do Plants Need Sunshine?

Name _____

What You Need:
- 3 pots (or plastic cups)
- potting soil
- rye grass seeds
- water
- paper bag

What To Do:

1. Fill each pot with the potting soil.

2. Sprinkle rye grass seeds in each pot and cover with more soil.

3. Water each pot until the soil is wet.

4. Put one pot in a sunny window and water as needed.

Put one pot in a sunny window and DO NOT provide any additional water.

Put one pot in a dark cupboard and cover with a paper bag. Water this plant as needed.

5. Keep an eye on the plants and see what happens to each plant over the course of the week.

? Next Question

What happens if you place all three plants in the same sunny location and provide them with water?

 Notebook Reflection

What three things do all plants need in order to grow and to be healthy and strong? What happens to the plant if one of the necessary items is missing?

How Much Can I Breathe?

Name _____

What You Need: • a clock   • a bendable straw

               • a sink or a tote bin   • a two-liter bottle

What To Do:

1. Find a partner.

2. Choose one person to hold his or her breath. The other person will count the time.

3. One person takes a deep breath, pinches her nose, and holds her breath for as long as she can. It is okay if she does not hold it very long. The other person counts the time.

4. Write your time. _____

5. Switch roles.

6. Write your partner's time. _____

7. Why do you need to breathe?

_____

_____

8. Fill a sink or a tote bin with water.

9. Fill up the two-liter bottle with water. Tip it upside down with the neck under the water.

What To Do: *(cont.)*

10. Put the tip of the straw under the neck of the bottle. It should look the pictures to the right.

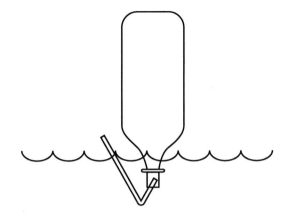

11. First, make a guess: How much water will you blow out? Draw your prediction on the bottle:

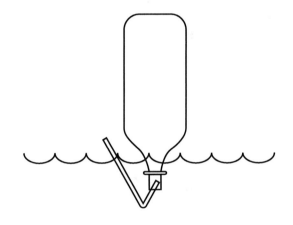

12. Choose one person to hold the bottle. The other person takes a deep breath and blows into the straw.

13. Draw the new water line on the bottle:

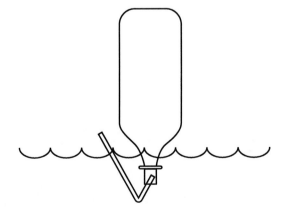

What To Do: *(cont.)*

14. Switch roles. Draw your partner's water line on the bottle:

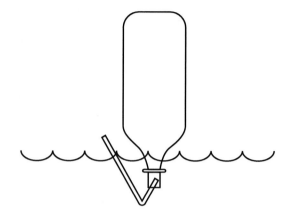

15. Which one of you pushed out more water?

_____

16. Did you push out more or less than you thought you would?

_____

_____

_____

❓ Next Question

If you were much bigger, do you think you would blow out more or less water?

How much water do you think a small animal, like a cat, could blow out?

Notebook Reflection

Get together with another pair. Write down how long each one of you held your breath. Did each one hold his or her breath the same length of time? Why do you think this is?

How Far Can Plants Reach?

Name _____

What You Need:
- see-through plastic cups
- seeds
- potting soil
- wooden craft sticks or tongue depressors
- ruler
- water

What To Do:

1. Fill a cup two-thirds full with potting soil.

2. Along the sides of the cup, place four seeds at different depths: 2 cm, 4 cm, 6 cm, and 8 cm (1 in., 2 in., 3 in., 4 in.) from the top of the soil. (Place the ruler by the side of the cup and use a craft stick to push the seed down to the correct depth.)

3. Make sure the seed is covered with soil. Then sprinkle water in each cup.

4. Place the cups in a sunny window and water as needed for two weeks. Draw what you see.

How Far Can Plants Reach? *(cont.)*

What To Do: *(cont.)*

 Next Question

What would happen if a different number of seeds (2 seeds, 5 seeds, 10 seeds, 20 seeds) were placed in each cup? Which cup of seeds do you think would grow the best? Why?

Notebook Reflection

Which plant grew the best? Why do you think that is?

What Is in My Square Meter Now?

Name _____

What You Need:
- ruler
- pegs
- string
- themometer
- specimen containers
- digital camera

What To Do:

1. Go outside and find a place with some vegetation.

2. Use the ruler to accurately measure one square meter.

3. Push one peg into each corner of the square meter. Tie string around the pegs to mark the perimeter.

4. Take a photograph or draw a detailed map of your square meter.

5. Draw up an observation sheet on a separate piece of paper. Record the date, the temperature, weather conditions, each type of vegetation and the number of each type, each type of mini-beast and the number of each type.

6. On your observation sheet, draw and label a detailed diagram of each different thing you see.

7. Also draw a map of your square meter.

8. Make up a key for each type of vegetation and mini-beast. Use the key to show the location of each type of vegetation and mini-beast.

9. Compare your findings with those of your classmates. Put the results into a whole class data entry sheet.

10. Summarize the average class results.

 Next Question

Does weather and time of day affect your results? Do the lab again at a different time of day.

 Notebook Reflection

How are your results similar to the average class results? How are they different?

Diversity of Life

This chapter provides activities that address McREL Science Standard 7.

Student understands biological evolution and the diversity of life.

Knows that some kinds of organisms that once lived on Earth have completely disappeared (e.g., dinosaurs, trilobites, mammoths, horsetail trees)	What Are Fossils?, page 107 What Were Dinosaurs Like?, page 109
Knows that there are similarities and differences in the appearance and behavior of plants and animals	How Can I Group Seeds?, page 110 Where Are Mini-Beasts?, page 111 Can You Find My Grass?, page 113 What Do Mini-Beasts Look Like Up Close?, see Teacher CD

How to Teach Diversity of Life

The Diversity of Life

There is a great deal of confusion as to how to organize all the living things on the planet. With ten million known species and millions more unknown species, that's hardly a surprise.

Morphological Classification

In the 1700s a Swedish scientist named Carl von Linné (or Carolus Linnaeus) invented a system to make sense of the way scientists group and name living things. The system is based on how similar and different living things are. He placed them in groups.

The groups contained organisms that look similar or have things in common. The largest groups are called kingdoms. Plants formed one kingdom; animals formed a separate kingdom. If it didn't move, it was a plant; if it moved, it was an animal. Linnaeus also had a third kingdom for minerals, which has since been discarded. New kingdoms have also been introduced—fungi were split off from plants, microorganisms from plant and animal kingdoms were regrouped into protoctista, bacteria, and archaea. Today there are six kingdoms.

The smallest groups are species—cows, tigers, and oak trees are all examples of species. Species are unique. Members of a species are a bit like the aristocracy; they breed with one another but (in normal circumstances) they can't breed with anyone else!

In between are phyla or divisions, classes, orders, families, and genera.

Linnaeus gave each species a two-part name. The two parts work like your surname and first name. They tell you which genus and species each living thing is. The ancient language of Latin is used for the names. This is so that everyone can understand them, no matter which language they normally speak. For example, the Latin name for a tiger is Panthera tigris. The genus is Panthera and the species is tigris. The scientific names are given group names first. Think of some student names and reverse them: Smith, Sharon, for example. Notice that the first, or generic, name always has a capital letter. The specific name always has a lower case initial letter. For example, Homo sapiens.

Cladism

However, morphological classification has some significant drawbacks. Since it is based on body structure, it groups organisms that look alike together. However, the fact that two organisms look similar is no guarantee that they actually live or behave in similar ways.

Cladism is an approach in which biologists group organisms based on their genetic ancestors. By studying DNA and evolutionary development, biologists are able to more precisely map how organisms came to be the way they are today.

The basic unit, the clade, is the group of organisms that share a single common ancestor. It includes all organisms that are descended from that ancestor.

Cladism and morphological classification overlap, and a great deal of developing science involves adapting morphological classifications to map to clades. For instance, all birds share a common ancestor, Archaeopteryx, and all descendants of Archaeopteryx are birds. Their class, Aves, is also a clade.

However, the reptile class Sauropsida is different. All of these organisms share a common ancestor—some proto-reptile of distant past—but not all of that proto-

reptile's descendants are in Sauropsida. There's a big group missing: the birds! Sauropsida is not a clade, but Sauropsida and Aves together are a clade.

Adaption

Only humans can adapt to almost any habitat. By wearing special clothes, living in special shelters or using technology, humans can live at the North Pole or in a desert, can go underwater, or can fly.

Each plant and each animal suits the place where it lives. You don't find monkeys under the sea or fish up trees. Monkeys and fish are adapted to their habitats.

An adaptation is a change in the way that plants or animals are shaped that suits them to their habitat. For example, while the eagle cannot reach the nectar inside flowers, it can soar high in the sky, has wonderful eyesight to help it spot its prey and fierce talons and a beak to catch it. The hummingbird cannot catch and eat other birds, but it is so tiny and has such an amazing speed of wing flapping that it can hover over flowers to feed on the nectar (and it can fly backwards—the only bird that can!).

Many animals fly but they fly in different ways. Hawkmoths can fly at 45 km an hour to escape predators. Swifts have small wings, adapted to flying at 170 km an hour to catch flying insects. Albatross don't fly so fast. Their huge wings—up to four meters across—are adapted to enable them to soar and glide for long periods.

All these different flying animals are adapted to living in different habitats. Each exploits its own environmental niche—usually very successfully, until some human comes along and messes it up.

What Are Fossils?

Name _____

What You Need:

- a small plastic dinosaur
- 120 mL (1/2 c.) liquid gelatin
- a craft stick
- an old, clean toothbrush
- 150 mL (8 oz.) styrofoam cup
- a marker
- a plate

What To Do:

1. Get a dinosaur and a cup.

2. Write your name on your cup.

3. Put your dinosaur in it.

4. The dinosaurs died. Sand and dirt covered them. Time passed. The dinosaur's bones became hard like rocks. The colored gelatin is like the sand and dirt.

5. Add the liquid colored gelatin to your cup.

6. Place your cup in the refrigerator.

7. Wait two hours.

8. Get a plate, a brush, and a craft stick.

9. Draw what you see:

What To Do: *(cont.)*

10. Use the craft stick to slide the colored gelatin out of the cup.

11. Archaeologists use tools and brushes to dig fossils from rocks. They are gentle. They do not want to chip the fossil. Use your tools to free the dinosaur fossil.

12. Draw your dinosaur:

 Next Question

Have you ever seen a fossil?

Where did you find it?

Was it a plant or an animal?

What kind?

Notebook Reflection

When all of one kind of animal dies, the animal is extinct. There are no more of them. There never will be. Draw an extinct animal in your science notebook.

What Were Dinosaurs Like?

Name _____

What You Need:

- pictures of dinosaurs
- science-related video on dinosaurs
- shoeboxes
- scrap box arts and crafts supplies including: construction paper, yarn, popsicle sticks, etc.
- glue
- scissors
- clean sheets of paper
- crayons or markers
- poster paint
- paint brushes
- potting soil
- small rocks
- clay

What To Do:

1. Watch the video about dinosaurs and examine the pictures of dinosaurs. On another page, draw what you liked the most about the dinosaurs you saw.

2. Paint the inside of the shoebox to resemble what the earth looked like when dinosaurs were alive.

3. Once the paint has dried, add various elements to recreate the dinosaurs' habitats. Remember to include trees, rocks, soil, water, etc.

4. Using the clay, make a model of one of the dinosaurs. Place the dinosaur in its habitat.

 **Next Question**

What would life be like on earth if dinosaurs were still alive? How would both people and dinosaurs survive?

 Notebook Reflection

How is Earth different today than when dinosaurs roamed the land?

How Can I Group Seeds?

Name _____

What You Need: • lots of different seeds • brown paper
• blue paper • green paper
• red paper • yellow paper

What To Do:

1. Count and record the number of seeds that you have.

   I have _____ seeds.

2. Sort the seeds into two groups. Put round seeds on the red paper. Put seeds that are not round on the blue paper.

3. Count and record the number of seeds in each group.

   I have _____ round seeds.

   I have _____ seeds that aren't round.

4. Now, take all the round seeds. Sort them into three groups. Put brown round seeds on the brown paper. Put green round seeds on the green paper. Put round seeds of other colors on the yellow paper.

5. Count and record the number of seeds in each group.

   I have _____ brown round seeds.

   I have _____ green round seeds.

   I have _____ round seeds of other colors.

 **Next Question**

How could you sort the seeds that are not round?

 Notebook Reflection

Why would different plants have differently shaped seeds?

Where Are Mini-Beasts?

Name _____

What You Need:
- small spade
- white paper
- 30 cm x 30 cm (1 ft. x 1 ft.) frame

What To Do:

1. Sit in a circle outside in a place where you might find mini-beasts. What time of day is it? What is the weather like?

_____

_____

_____

2. Look up at the sky. Draw and count the mini-beasts you see there.

What To Do: *(cont.)*

3. Put the frame on the ground. Draw and count the mini-beasts that you see inside the frame.

4. Dig the ground inside the frame. Put the soil on white paper. Draw and count the mini-beasts you find in the soil.

5. Put the soil and mini-beasts back where they came from.

 **Next Question**

Do you find different mini-beasts during different parts of the day? What about during different weather?

 Notebook Reflection

Imagine you are a mini-beast. What would your day be like? What other mini-beasts would you meet?

Can You Find My Grass?

Name _____

What You Need:
- plant specimen
- water
- trowel
- resealable bag

What To Do:

1. Get a number from your teacher. You should be the only student with that number in the class. Do not write your number on this page.

2. Find your specimen somewhere on the school grounds. Carefully dig out the plant and the dirt around it. Make sure the roots are still on the plant.

3. Wash the dirt away from the roots so that you can see the whole plant.

4. Put your plant in the resealable bag. Write your number on the bag.

5. Draw your plant in the box below.

Can You Find My Grass? *(cont.)*

What To Do: *(cont.)*

6. Put your plant specimen on the table with the other specimens.

7. Swap your drawing with a partner. Use the drawing to find the matching specimen on the table. Write the number of the specimen that you think your partner used. _____

8. Trade your drawing back. Did you guess correctly? Did your partner?

My guess was _____.

My partner's guess was _____.

9. Were either of you right? _____

 **Next Question**

How would you make matching drawings and specimens easier?

 Notebook Reflection

What was easy about matching the drawing to the specimen? What was difficult?

Matter

This chapter provides activities that address McREL Science Standard 8.

Student understands the structure and properties of matter.

Knows that different objects are made up of many different types of materials (e.g., cloth, paper, wood, metal) and have many different observable properties (e.g., color, size, shape, weight)	What Can Goop do?, page 121 How Is Paper Made?, page 122
Knows that things can be done to materials to change some of their properties (e.g., heating, freezing, mixing, cutting, dissolving, bending), but not all materials respond the same way to what is done to them	How Can I Make an Egg Grow?, page 124 How Do Things Melt?, page 126 How Does Dough Work?, page 127 Where Does a Wet Handprint Go?, page 129 How Are Things Different?, page 131 Does It Float?, page 133 How Does Fruit Float?, see Teacher CD How Are Textiles Different?, see Teacher CD Do Different Textiles Get Clean Easier?, see Teacher CD How Tough Are Textiles?, see Teacher CD How Strong Are Textiles?, see Teacher CD

How to Teach Matter

The world is full of stuff. In fact, it's made from stuff—including you, me, and this book. Scientists call this stuff matter—a confusing word if you are a student being told that something "doesn't matter." Because in the scientific sense, matter is the substance of the universe. It's all the stuff in the world: rocks, wood, plastic, and steel. It's rare and expensive, like gold and diamonds, or common and cheap, like soil and water. It's everywhere. Different materials have different properties.

By looking at the properties of materials, how they are used, and how they might be changed, this subject prepares students for their later understanding of chemistry.

It is important to tackle work on matter in a logical order. Only then can students understand that materials differ; that they can be grouped and classified in many ways; that this classification can help us to choose the right materials for a task; and finally, that there are ways of changing materials that make them suitable for a range of needs and tasks.

Particle Theory

Particle theory is simply the idea that everything is made up of very tiny bits, or particles. An understanding of this is enormously helpful when learning about materials. And it isn't difficult to understand.

A selection of great and good scientists were asked to imagine that all the science knowledge in the world was to be destroyed but they could save one piece of information. What would it be? Almost without exception, they chose the same idea—rejecting evolution, electricity, and Newton's laws of motion. The fact they wanted to pass on to succeeding generations was that all matter is made up of tiny particles.

Words like "atom," "molecule," and "particle" are in general use—sometimes correctly, sometimes not. Most young students could make a stab at explaining what particles are, or at least that they are "very, very small bits." Some might even know that they are mostly space. Understanding what particles are is a great help to understanding the behavior of materials.

Atoms

An atom is the smallest particle of a material that still retains the characteristics of that material. That is, a bar of iron is made of iron. Cut off a piece, and it's still iron. Cut off a piece of that piece, and it's still iron. You can keep cutting and cutting until you've got just one single iron atom—and it's still iron.

However, if you cut that atom in half, what you have ceases to be iron. What you would have is a collection of subatomic particles: protons, neutrons, and electrons. Now, if you really had split that iron atom, the subatomic particles would clump back together (after releasing a whole lot of fission energy) immediately. Those new groups of subatomic particles would be new atoms of different elements, no longer iron and no longer with the characteristics of that material.

Molecules

Molecules are groups of atoms which are chemically stuck together. The molecule often has different characteristics than the molecules that went into it. Sodium and chlorine, for instance, are quite poisonous—but sodium chloride, also known as table salt, is essential to human life.

How to Teach Matter *(cont.)*

Solid, Liquid, and Gas

Materials can be divided into solids, liquids, and gases. This isn't as easy as it sounds. There are some materials that behave in ways that put them in more than one group. Water, for example, can be found in all three states. In addition, it's very hard to prove to students that gases exist.

- If the particles are closely bonded together—able to vibrate but not part from each other—then the material is a solid.

- If the particles are close but not packed, so that they can move around, the material is a liquid.

- If the particles are widely spaced and move around, occasionally crashing into one another, the material is a gas.

These three are called the states of matter.

Changes with Temperature

The changes between the three states of matter are connected to changes in temperature. Increase the temperature, and a solid becomes a liquid, or a liquid a gas. Very occasionally, a solid becomes a gas without a liquid stage. Reduce the temperature, and gas becomes a liquid, or a liquid solidifies.

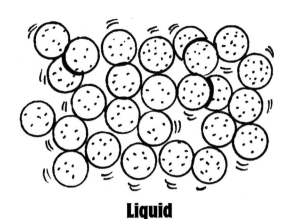

Liquid

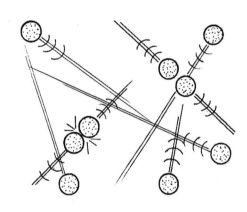

Gas

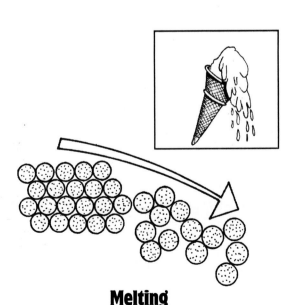

Melting

Solid

How to Teach Matter *(cont.)*

Fascinating Facts

And Glass Is a Liquid

Let's just get this one out of the way. It comes up later, but it's a favorite in trivia contests and among well-read students. Glass is a liquid.

Liquids flow. The thicker the liquid, the slower the flow. At room temperature, water flows freely while syrup flows slowly. Syrup has a higher viscosity than water. It takes an age to flow from the bottle. But glass has an even higher viscosity than syrup. You can't imagine windows made from syrup. But glass has such a high viscosity— it is so thick—that you can cut it into sheets and put it into windows. Over time, it flows downward. Clear evidence of thickening can be seen at the bottom of century-old windows. The bottom of the pane is thicker than the top.

Melting and Freezing

When solids melt, they become liquids. They can flow, pour, and fill a shape. Some solids melt when they are heated. Butter melts to become a liquid. Chocolate melts, too. Both become solid again when they are cooled. The cooling process is called freezing—even if it's not very cold to you or me.

Chocolate is not changed much by the melting, but butter loses water when it melts. The butter is changed by the melting. You can't change it back.

Evaporation and Condensation

Evaporation is the process by which a liquid turns into a gas. Extra heat jostles the liquid molecules around until they're so excited, they don't even stick together any more. They're now a gas.

Condensation is a process by which a vapor or a gas turns back to a liquid. Water vapor condenses on a cold window and collects in a liquid form again.

Changing Matter

The concept of materials changing is a difficult one. It's not surprising that students recognize changes when they are spectacular—a color change, a flame, smoke—but not when they are unexciting.

They may feel that "stuff disappears." There was a match, it was lit, and now it's gone. They may think that the product was somehow inside the original material—thus rust may be thought to ooze out of a corroding nail. They may simply think that one material has "turned into" another—the flour and water have turned into bread—without a word of explanation.

Sometimes we need to bring the material back to show that it was there all along.

Can You Make Bread from Toast?

Matter changes in two ways: physically and chemically. The difference between physical and chemical change is that whereas physical change is only a change in form—the substance is still there—chemical change is when new and irreversible substances are created. Sugar dissolving in tea is a physical change, but baking a cake is a chemical change.

How to Teach Matter *(cont.)*

Some physical changes are irreversible. Try sawing your leg off to see what I mean. No chemical change has taken place, but reattachment could be difficult.

So think of it this way:

Physical changes involve the rearrangement of particles: mixing, separating, putting them in a different state (solid, liquid, gas), or otherwise doing something to them without actually changing the particles themselves.

Chemical changes give you something new. The particles have been changed by splitting or combining with others or by changing partners so that they produce a new material you didn't have before.

So making sawdust is a physical change (which is irreversible), but making ammonia from hydrogen and nitrogen is a chemical change which is reversible—you can get the hydrogen and nitrogen back.

Although most physical changes are reversible and most chemical changes are not, there are exceptions!

Toast some bread. What kind of change happens? Can you reverse it? What is the material that forms on the surface of the bread? Burned toast is carbon. That's a new material, so the change is a chemical one. If you cut your toast in half, though, that change is physical—no new materials are made; the toast is just in two parts instead of one.

Does Salt Disappear in Water?

If you ask students what happens when something dissolves, they will often tell you that it "disappears." This seems to be true of materials that dissolve to make a colorless liquid—like salt or sugar.

But dissolving instant coffee produces a material where the coffee has far from disappeared—it is clearly there throughout the changed, colored liquid.

Students' views may reflect their observations. Consider the following: "When I add sugar to my tea, it just disappears. You see the same thing when you add salt to water; first it's there and then it's not. The water won't weigh any more with the salt in it—it's just disappeared. You could go on adding salt if you liked. It would just go on filling the spaces."

Dissolving takes place when one substance is dispersed through another to become a single material. This material is called a solution. In theory, the substances involved could be solids, liquids, or gases. In practice, students will come across this most often when they add something solid to a liquid—for example, salt to water or sugar to tea. The solid and the liquid are called the solute and the solvent.

When a solid dissolves, it becomes dispersed throughout the liquid. If you were to sample any part of the liquid, you would find the solid there. This is not what happens when you add something insoluble to liquid (when it lies at the bottom or floats on the top) or something that forms a suspension, like flour (where the bits float about until they sometimes sink to the bottom).

When a white or colorless solid is added to water, it appears to disappear. Tasting safe materials in solution proves that the solid is still there. Colored solids may color the water, and the students can see how they color the whole of the solvent evenly.

How to Teach Matter *(cont.)*

Diffusion

Open a new air freshener, put it on a table, and then walk around the room. How quickly does the smell fill the room? Where do you have to stand so that you cannot smell it? Everything is made up of tiny particles. They are closely packed in solids, freer to move in liquids and freest of all in gases. How does that explain your air freshener?

The solid material in the freshener is losing particles. The particles are floating off and arriving in your nose, an organ designed to accept the tiny particles in a gas. Although your nose isn't in direct contact with the air freshener, you know it is in the room!

Can't Take Any More!

When the solvent cannot dissolve any more of the solute—the water cannot dissolve any more salt, for example—then the solution is saturated. Students may observe that salt will not go on dissolving in water forever. You can increase the amount of solute that the solvent will dissolve by raising the temperature of the solution, but as soon as the temperature falls, the solid comes out of solution again.

Raising the temperature of the solute and stirring are familiar ways of speeding up dissolving. These two methods work because both encourage the release of the tiny particles of solid into the liquid. As a student once said when explaining dissolving, "If you dropped me in hot water and then hit me around the head with a spoon, I'd let go of my friends, too!"

Dissolving should not be confused with melting. Melting is the change of state from solid to liquid with increased temperature. Dissolving is one substance dispersing into another substance. However, some materials melt and dissolve simultaneously. Jelly can become a liquid and disperse through the water when stirred with hot water.

What Really Happens?

What happens to things that dissolve? Surely the salt has to go somewhere? When you add a solid that will dissolve to a liquid, it begins by filling the spaces between the particles of liquid. Rather like a theater with a fixed number of seats, the liquid will take so many arrivals before it is full. When it is full, the liquid can take no more, and is said to be saturated. The excess, like disappointed film-goers, is rejected and sinks to the bottom. Strangely, the level of the solute actually falls at first.

But some materials, like sand, don't dissolve. They may sink to the bottom of the liquid or, if they are low density, they may sit in mid-water or in suspension. If you put the liquid through a filter, only dissolved particles pass through. Large, undissolved particles are netted and stay behind. If you then let the water evaporate, you will be left with the dissolved solid, which may form crystals.

What Can Goop Do?

Name _____

What You Need:
- 250 mL (8 oz.) plastic cup
- 15 mL (1 Tbsp.) of liquid starch
- 30 mL (2 Tbsps) of white glue
- food coloring (optional)
- wooden craft stick or tongue depressor

What To Do:

1. In the cup mix together all of the ingredients (including the food coloring) and let the mixture stand for 5 minutes. Stir the ingredients again and let stand for 5 minutes. For the third and final time, stir the ingredients and let stand for 5 minutes.

2. Is the goop a solid or a liquid? _____

3. Does it pour easily from one cup to another? _____

4. Can it hold the shape of a ball or a cube? _____

5. What happens when it is poked by a craft stick?

   _____

6. What happens when it is poured out onto the table?

   _____

   _____

Next Question

Repeat the experiment, but use different amounts of ingredients. Be sure to label the amounts that go into each batch of goop. How are the new goops the same and different?

Notebook Reflection

Pretend you are goop. How do you feel being poured from one cup to another, being rolled into a ball or a cube, and being poked by a craft stick? Tell about your life as goop.

How Is Paper Made?

Name _____

What You Need:

- aluminum foil in 15 cm (6 in.) squares
- scissors
- pencil
- newspaper
- large jar with lid
- hot tap water
- wooden spoon
- metal baking pans
- cornstarch
- measuring cup
- markers, crayons, or paint

What To Do:

1. Use a pencil to punch holes in each foil square. The holes should be in vertical rows about 1 cm (1/2 in.) apart.

2. Cut or tear the newspaper into smaller pieces. You want to pack the jar half-full with shredded paper.

3. Put the paper into the jar and fill the jar about 3/4 of the way with hot tap water. Put the lid on the jar and let the jar stand for about three hours. Every once in a while go and shake the jar or stir the jar to break up the clumpy paper. Add more hot tap water as the paper absorbs the water already in the jar.

4. Once the newspaper has become a soupy, creamy mixture, pour the mixture into the baking pans. Add more hot water. Stir the mixture to make sure all of the paper has dissolved.

5. Get a 100 mL (1/2 cup) of hot tap water and add 40 mL (3 Tbsps) of cornstarch. Stir the mixture until all of the cornstarch has dissolved. Pour the mixture over the paper in the baking pan.

What To Do: *(cont.)*

6. Place a foil square over the mixture in the baking pan. Press down on the foil square. Then pull the foil up. Some of the mixture should stick to the foil.

7. Place the foil square on the table and press it flat to squeeze out all of the water. Repeat this same step with the three other foil squares.

8. Let the foil-backed paper dry in the sun on clean sheets of newspaper. Continue to squeeze any extra water out of the foil. If you see any holes or tears in the paper, pinch the sides of the hole or tear together.

9. After three hours, carefully peel the paper from the foil back. Trim the paper into a square notecard. Use crayons, markers, or paint to decorate the notecard.

10. Try this same experiment using clean sheets of white paper instead of newspaper. What do you notice is different about the feel, look, and texture of the paper?

Next Question

What could you do to make colored paper?

Notebook Reflection

Write about the experiment in your science notebook. What did you learn about making paper?

How Can I Make an Egg Grow?

Name _____

What You Need:
- 2 eggs
- water
- vinegar
- 2 plastic cups

What To Do:

1. Place one egg in each cup.
2. Fill one cup with water. Fill the other cup with vinegar.
3. Leave the cups in a safe place where they can't be spilled.
4. After two hours, look at the eggs. Have they changed?

_____

_____

5. Touch the egg in the vinegar. What does it look and feel like?

_____

_____

6. Leave the eggs for five days. Record their sizes each day.

Day 1

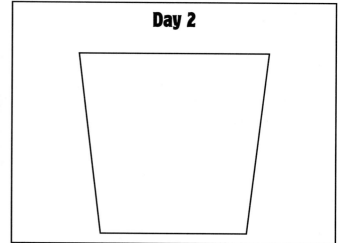

Day 2

How Can I Make an Egg Grow? *(cont.)*

 **What To Do:** *(cont.)*

Day 3

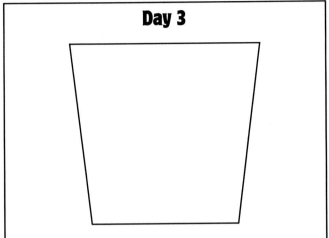

Day 4

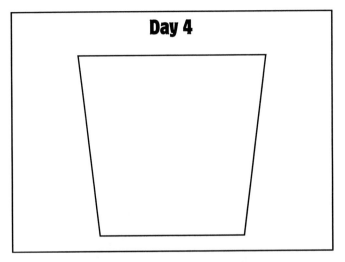

Day 5

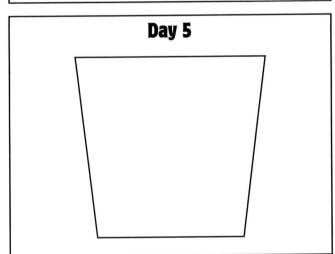

7. After five days, feel both eggs. Circle the words that describe the egg in the vinegar. Underline the words to describe the egg in the water.

Word Bank:	
soft	bouncy
clear	pointy
round	little
hard	smooth
bumpy	slimy
stretched	hard

 Next Question

What happens if you put a chicken bone in a jar of vinegar for five days?

Notebook Reflection

What do you think happened to the egg shell? Where did it go?

How Do Things Melt?

Name _____

What You Need:
- butter
- candle wax
- chocolate
- sugar
- foil
- craft stick
- heat source

What To Do:

1. Cut out four squares of foil.

2. Fold the edges up to make flat trays.

3. Place the small amount of butter in the first tray, candle wax in the second tray, chocolate in the third tray, and sugar in the fourth tray.

4. Switch on the heat source. Point it onto the trays.

5. Watch for five minutes to see what happens to each substance. Draw what happens.

6. Switch off the heat source. Carefully stir each substance with the craft stick.

7. Let them cool. What happens? _____

_____

 **Next Question**

Put some sugar in a metal spoon. Ask your teacher to light a candle. Hold the spoon over the candle. What happens?

 Notebook Reflection

How did the different substances react to heat? How did they react differently? The same?

How Does Dough Work?

Name _____

What You Need:
- 700 mL (3 c.) flour
- 475 mL (2 c.) salt
- bowl
- 120 mL (1/2 c.) vegetable oil
- wooden spoon
- water
- baking tray
- paper
- oven

What To Do:

1. Mix the flour and salt in the bowl.

2. Add the oil and mix it in with the wooden spoon.

3. Pour in water and stir until the mixture sticks together.

4. Roll the mixture into a ball. Divide it among your group.

5. Make a shape or a creature out of your mixture.

6. Place your shape or creature on a piece of paper on the baking tray. Draw your shape.

How Does Dough Work? *(cont.)*

What To Do: *(cont.)*

7. Your teacher will bake the shape in the oven at 80° C (180° F) for 10 minutes. What happens to the shape?

 Next Question

What other recipes change the food when you cook it?

Notebook Reflection

Can you turn your shape back into flour, salt, oil, and water? How or why?

Where Does a Wet Handprint Go?

Name _____

What You Need:
- water
- saucer
- chalkboard
- towel

What To Do:

1. Pour some water in the saucer and leave it on the window sill. Predict what will happen to the water in the saucer after five days. Draw what happens each day.

2. Get your hand wet. Make a handprint on the chalkboard. Draw what happens over the next five minutes.

Where Does a Wet Handprint Go? *(cont.)*

 **What To Do:** *(cont.)*

3. What happened to the handprint?

_____

_____

4. Where did the water go?

_____

_____

_____

 **Next Question**

How could you make this happen faster? How could you make it happen slower?

 Notebook Reflection

Imagine you are the handprint. Describe what happens to you as time passes.

How Are Things Different?

Name _____

What You Need:

- ruler
- rubber band
- metal paper clip
- pencil
- eraser
- sock
- penny
- marble
- ball
- 5 cm × 5 cm (2 in. × 2 in.) foil square

What To Do:

1. Fill in the chart.

	Draw it	What is it made of?	What color?	Does it stretch?	Is it shiny?
Rubber band					
Paper clip					
Pencil					
Eraser					
Sock					
foil					
Penny					
Marble					
Ball					

 **What To Do:** (cont.)

2. Draw two things that have the same shape.

3. Draw two things that stretch.

What are these things made of?

_____

_____

4. What are the paper clip and foil made of? _____

What color are they? _____

Are they both shiny? _____

 Next Question

Your clothes are made of cloth. Look at your chart. Socks are made of cloth, too. Tug gently on your shirt. Does it stretch like the sock?

 Notebook Reflection

Pick two things from the chart. Draw a picture of each. Make a T-chart. List the ways these things are alike. List the ways these things are different.

Does It Float?

Name _____

What You Need:

- large plastic mixing bowl
- water
- rubber band
- paper clip
- pencil
- piece of paper
- marble
- ice cube
- cork
- candle
- pumice stone
- rock
- 5 cm × 5 cm (2 in. × 2 in.) foil square
- leaf

What To Do:

1. Find a partner. Get a mixing bowl.
2. Fill the bowl halfway with water.
3. Draw pictures of the items that you think will float.

Does It Float? *(cont.)*

What To Do: *(cont.)*

4. One at a time, put each thing into the bowl. If it stays at the top, then it floats. If it goes to the bottom, the thing sinks.

5. Fill in the chart.

	Float	Sink
Rubber band		
Paper clip		
Pencil		
Paper		
Marble		
Ice cube		
Cork		
Candle		
Pumice stone		
Rock		
Aluminum foil		
Leaf		

 **Next Question**

Fold up the edges of the foil so it looks like a boat. Does it float? Crush the foil into a ball. Does it float now? Why?

 Notebook Reflection

Draw two bowls. In one, draw the things that float. In the other, draw the things that sink.

Energy

This chapter provides activities that address McREL Science Standard 9.

Student understands the sources and properties of energy.

Knows that the Sun supplies heat and light to Earth	How Fast Do Clothes Dry?, page 141 How Can I Use the Sun to Cook?, page 143 How Can I Use the Sun?, see Teacher CD
Knows that heat can be produced in many ways (e.g., burning, rubbing, mixing substances together)	Can I Make the Snake Dance?, page 145 How Can I Make Heat?, page 146 How Can I Cut a String Without Scissors?, page 148
Knows that electricity in circuits can produce light, heat, sound, and magnetic effects	How Do I Use Electricity?, page 149 How Can I Light a Lightbulb?, page 150 How Can a Battery Make Heat?, page 151 How Can a Fruit Make Electricity?, page 152 How Does a Flashlight Work?, page 153
Knows that sound is produced by vibrating objects	What Is Sound Made of?, page 155 How Is a Kazoo Made?, page 158 How Can I Make Noise?, page 159 How Does a Voice Box Work?, see Teacher CD
Knows that light travels in a straight line until it strikes an object	How Do Shadows Work?, page 160

How to Teach Energy

Students will have a great deal of experience with energy but a difficult time identifying what energy they encounter every day. Many will suggest electricity, but they also encounter heat, light, and sound every minute of every day of their lives.

Heat and Temperature

Temperature is a measure of how hot something is, not how much heat there is in it. A bucket of hot water may have considerable heat in it, but it is not at the same high temperature as a light bulb or a sparkler firework.

Thermometers measure the level of heat in degrees. There have been several scales for measuring temperature, but the most common is the Celsius scale, named after Anders Celsius. This scale calls the freezing point of water 0° C, and the boiling point of water 100° C.

If the sun is shining through the windows, or the heat is on, you may be warm. If the windows and doors are open, and the heat is off, you may be feeling chilly. If you have a thick sweater on, you may be warm, even if the room is cold. Several factors determine how cold you may feel—how cold the room is, how warm your body is, and how warm the heater is. To know each of these factors, we have to compare temperatures with the temperature of our bodies. However, our bodies are not accurate measuring instruments.

You can see this for yourself by conducting the following short experiment. Fill three bowls with water. Fill one from the hot tap (not too hot!), one from the cold tap, and one using half hot and half cold water. Put your bowls in a row: hot, warm, and cold. Put one hand in the hot water and one in the cold. Count to ten. Now put both hands in the warm water.

What do you notice? Because one hand has become used to hot water and the other to cold, they don't do a very good job of telling you how warm the warm water is. Why is using your body a poor way of measuring temperature? While a thermometer will give you an objective measure, based on a defined scale, your hands relate the temperature to previous experiences. The hand that has been in cold water senses the warm water as hot. The hand that has been in hotter water senses the warm water as cold. We have all had this sort of experience in the swimming pool, moving from toddler pool to main pool, from pool to hot shower. The sea can also feel very cold after you have been sitting on a warm beach.

Light

Light is a form of energy. The energy of light is called radiant energy. To radiate means to send out rays or waves. Only a certain type of radiant energy can be seen with the human eye. We call this visible light.

We can see because of light. Light bounces off objects and travels to our eyes. Our eyes and brain work together to translate that light into what we see.

How Light Is Made

Everything is made of very tiny particles: atoms and molecules. Heat causes particles to become excited and move faster. The excited particles then radiate light.

Have you ever seen the bottom of a pan that is heating on the stove? Did it look like the hot pan was turning colors? When heated, the atoms on the surface of the pan start to bump into each other. This causes them to give off extra energy. This radiant energy is what scientists call light.

Light travels in waves much like water moves in waves. The amount of energy that a wave carries determines the color of the light. Waves differ from each other in length, rate, and size. These are called wavelength, frequency, and amplitude. Wavelength relates to the color of the light.

What happens when a light wave hits the atoms that make up everything? Several things might happen.

- The light can change direction, or refract.
- Some of the light rays can reflect off of the surface.
- The light can be absorbed into the material.

Refraction

Light rays bend as they travel through the surface of transparent material. Transparent means that light can be seen through it and move through it. This bend in the light is called refraction. It occurs when light travels through different materials at different speeds.

Reflection

The return of a wave of energy after it strikes a surface is called reflection. Smooth and polished surfaces like mirrors reflect more light than surfaces that are rough or bumpy.

When light reflects from a smooth surface, all of the light rays reflect in the same direction. A mirror is smooth, so you can see your image in it. When light reflects from a rough surface, the rays reflect in many directions. It is

impossible to see your reflection in paper, because the surface is rough.

Absorption

When it comes to color, absorption is the key. Look at the clothes you're wearing. What colors are they? The truth is, the colors are not in the clothing. The colors come from reflected and absorbed light. We see the colors because of the light that is reflected and sent to our eyes.

You know that light is made of waves. Each color has its own frequency. When visible light strikes an object, each frequency behaves differently. Some frequencies are absorbed. They are not seen. Some are reflected. The reflections are what appear as the color or colors of an object.

White light is made of all the colors of the rainbow. These colors are red, orange, yellow, green, blue, indigo, and violet. Some people know the colors as ROYGBIV. Now, look at something red. You can see just by looking at it that the object absorbs the frequencies for OYGBIV. But R, or red, is reflected. Your eyes pick up that reflection, and you see the object as red.

The important idea is that the color is not in the object. It is in the reflected light.

Sound

Sound comes from vibrations. Just like with light, atoms within substances move. Their movement creates sound waves. As the waves move through matter, they cause vibrations. The vibrations are picked up by the ear and sent as impulses to the brain. The brain translates them as the sounds we hear.

How to Teach Energy *(cont.)*

Sound Waves

Not all sound waves are alike. The differences let us hear various sounds. Scientists have discovered that sounds and sound waves differ in the following ways:

- Wavelength is the distance between the troughs on either side of a single wave.

- Amplitude is measured in the height of the sound wave. It relates to the loudness or softness of a sound. When a wave is high, the sound is loud, and the amplitude is large. When a wave is low, the amplitude is small and the sound is soft.

- Frequency of sound relates to speed. The number of cycles per second that waves pass a given location is the frequency. The brain understands frequency as pitch. Fast vibrations cause high pitch. Slower vibrations make lower-pitched sounds. A tweeting bird makes a high-pitched sound. A roaring lion makes a low-pitched sound.

The Speed of Sound

Sound waves pass through all forms of matter. These include gas, liquid, and solid. The speed of sound changes as the waves pass these different states of matter. Sound waves move:

- slowly through gases.

- more quickly through liquids.

- fastest through solids.

Temperature also affects the speed of moving sound waves. Higher temperatures cause sound to move faster. At normal room temperatures, sound travels about 343 meters per second. That is like traveling 1,217 kilometers per hour!

The Doppler Effect

As you've read, pitch is the highness or lowness of sound. The frequency of a sound determines its pitch. High-pitched sound has a higher frequency. Low-pitched sound has a lower frequency.

Have you ever noticed that the pitch of a fire truck's siren is high when it comes toward you? Then it is lower as it passes and moves away. What causes this?

As the fire truck approaches you, the waves reach you more frequently. The pitch is higher than if the fire truck were not moving.

This pitch change, which was caused by a moving object, is called the Doppler effect. The firefighters on the truck do not hear any change in pitch. Their distance from the source of the sound does not change. The Doppler effect only comes into play when the distance changes.

Electricity

How Does the Battery Work?

It's a common misconception that batteries are somehow full of electricity. Some students think that connecting them up in a circuit uses all this electricity up, and then the battery is empty or "dead." But that's not how it is.

Electricity is a flow of minute particles called electrons, passed hand to hand like "pass the parcel." These electrons are in the materials that make up the circuit, but the battery provides the "push" that makes the electrons flow.

The energy for the push of a battery comes from chemical reactions in the battery. It's when these chemicals have all changed and there is no longer the material for the chemical reaction that we say the battery is dead.

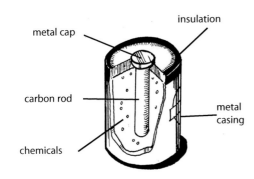

metal cap — insulation

carbon rod

chemicals

metal casing

Understanding the Flow of Electricity

The mistaken idea that electricity rushes out of the battery or the wall outlet, dashes to the radio, does its job, and disappears exhausted is not helped by the fact that a single cable operates most electrical appliances. Electricity apparently flows into the device to be "used up." You might show the students a piece of unconnected two-strand wire to show that electricity flows to a device and back again. There are two wires inside the cable.

The way electricity flows is affected by the components in the circuit. The electric current in a circuit is exactly the same wherever you decide to measure it. If there was electricity staggering back to the battery, you might expect there to be weak or strong points. But electricity flows a bit like water from a pump. The battery is the pump pushing the electricity around.

Complete Circuits

A circuit must be complete for the electricity to flow. All the components, linked in a complete circuit, are needed for a bulb in the circuit to light. Look closely at a flashlight bulb (when the light is off!). The wire filament inside is part of the circuit. The electricity flows right through the bulb.

Electric current has a direction from the negative to the positive terminal of the battery. When it was first investigated, it was thought that it flowed from positive to negative. However, this has now been shown not to be the case. And it certainly doesn't flow in both directions at once (the idea of "clashing currents" that students sometimes hold) despite the battery having two terminals.

An Analogy of an Electrical Circuit

You may need to use an analogy to explain the flow of electricity in a circuit to students. There is evidence that analogies help students to understand the invisible flow of electricity, but no analogy is perfect.

Use a loop of rope to represent the circuit. A student pushing the rope around in a circle represents the battery. If another student in the ring holds the rope more tightly, they create a resistance. They are behaving like a light bulb. An analogy of a switch would be a very tight grip on the rope: a resistance that no amount of pushing will overcome.

The bulb lights because the moving electrons collide with the fixed atoms in the thin filament wire (the filament wire resists the flow of the electrons). The moving electrons transfer energy from the battery to the bulb. The bulb glows—because it is in a glass globe that contains no oxygen, it can't burn away.

The wiring inside the bulb completes a full circuit. The more electricity flowing through the bulb, the brighter the bulb is. Students may think that a large battery will make a bulb brighter. Higher voltage batteries do tend to be larger, but size alone is not an indicator of voltage—for example, 1.5V batteries exist in several different sizes.

Caution!

It is essential to explain the safe use of wall outlet electricity devices early. Many students will have routine home experience of their use. Do not encourage exploration or investigation of wall outlet electricity. Explain that wall outlet electricity is dangerous and can be lethal.

How Fast Do Clothes Dry?

Name _____

What You Need:
- fan
- bowl of water
- 2 5-cm (2-in.) squares of cloth
- 2 drying racks

What To Do:

1. Find a partner. Together you will have four pieces of cloth.
2. Soak the cloth pieces in the water.
3. Wring them out to remove as much water as you can.
4. Lay one piece of cloth on a drying rack in the sun.
5. Lay one piece of cloth on a drying rack in a dark place.
6. Which piece do you think will dry first? Why?

   _____

   _____

   _____

7. Hang one piece of cloth on a drying rack. Point a fan at the rack. Turn it on. This is like wind.
8. Set up the other drying rack away from the fan. Hang the last piece of cloth on this rack.
9. Which piece of cloth do you think will dry first? Why?

   _____

   _____

   _____

How Fast Do Clothes Dry? *(cont.)*

What To Do: *(cont.)*

10. Check the pieces of cloth every 20 minutes. Draw the one that dried first in the spot where you put it to dry.

11. The cloth dried faster in the_____.

Circle one: sunny place / dark place

12. The cloth dried faster in the_____.

Circle one: still air / wind.

13. The sun_____ evaporate (dry up).

Circle one: helps water to / will not let water

 Next Question

What happens if you crumple the wet cloth into a ball and put it in the sun? Does it dry faster or slower than the cloth you laid flat? Why?

 Notebook Reflection

Draw a time line that shows which piece of cloth dries first, second, third, and last.

---

142 | #50163—*Science Labs: Standards-Based Investigations—K–2* | © *Shell Education*

How Can I Use the Sun to Cook?

Name _____

What You Need:

- a pizza box
- black construction paper
- some aluminum foil
- glue
- tape
- scissors

- clear plastic (like clear laminating film or clear plastic wrap)
- ruler
- felt tip marker
- straw

What To Do:

1. Draw a 3 cm (1 in.) border on the top of the pizza box.

2. Cut along three sides of the border. Do not cut the line running along the back of the box. (Have the teacher help you with the cutting.)

3. Make a flap by folding the top of the box back.

4. Line the flap with aluminum foil. Be sure to smooth out the wrinkles and then glue the foil into place.

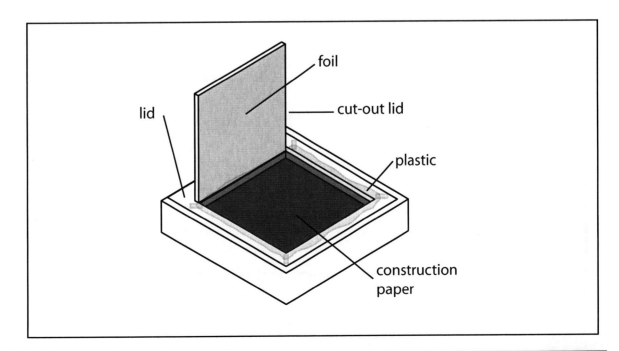

How Can I Use the Sun to Cook? *(cont.)*

What To Do: *(cont.)*

5. With the flap up, place plastic over the opening and tape the plastic to the bottom of the box. This will make a "window."

6. Line the bottom of the box with aluminum foil.

7. Cover the foil on the bottom of the box with black construction paper. Tape the construction paper into place.

8. Close the pizza box "window" and prop the flap (lid) open with a straw. Point the box towards the sun.

9. How long do you guess it will take to melt a handful of chocolate chips in the oven?

_____

_____

_____

_____

10. Test your guess. How long did it take?

_____

_____

 **Next Question**

How long does it take to melt a piece of chocolate onto a graham cracker? Can you adjust the oven to make it cook faster?

 Notebook Reflection

Why would a solar oven be useful?

Can I Make the Snake Dance?

Name _____

What You Need:
- cardstock
- scissors
- string
- lamp with light bulb

What To Do:

1. Cut a spiral shape out of the cardstock. This is the "snake."

2. Tie a length of string to the snake's tail.

3. Hold the snake over the warm light bulb being careful not to touch the light bulb with your body or with the snake.

4. What happens to the snake?

_____

_____

_____

_____

_____

? Next Question

What would happen if the snake were held over an extremely hot light bulb?

Notebook Reflection

Draw a picture of the snake dancing. Write several sentences describing how you made the snake dance.

How Can I Make Heat?

Name _____

What You Need:
- sandpaper
- block of wood
- rubber band

What To Do:

1. Rub your hands together as fast as you can.

2. Keep rubbing for 10 seconds. How do your hands feel?

_____

_____

_____

3. Get a piece of sandpaper and a block of wood.

4. Rub the wood with the sandpaper for 10 seconds. Stop. Touch the wood. How does it feel?

_____

_____

_____

5. Rubbing two things together makes them feel _____.
Circle one: *warmer / colder*

6. Put the rubber band around your thumb and index finger on both hands.

7. Quickly stretch the rubber band. Place a long section against your forehead. Does it feel warm? _____

How Can I Make Heat? *(cont.)*

What To Do: *(cont.)*

8. When you stretched the rubber band, the tiny parts that make up the rubber band rub against each other. Draw the way that the rubber band made heat.

 Next Question

Ask your parents how your home is heated.

 **Notebook Reflection**

Pretend that a friend is cold. Draw them a picture to show one way that he or she can warm up.

How Can I Cut a String Without Scissors?

Name _____

What You Need:
- length of string
- clear jar with lid
- tape
- magnifying glass

What To Do:

1. Tape one end of the string to the inside of the lid.

2. Put the lid back on the jar.

3. Place the jar in the sunlight. Hold a magnifying glass close to the jar so that the sun's rays are focused on the string.

4. What happens?

_____

_____

_____

 Next Question

What would it be like to have to use the sun's energy to cut everything you needed each day instead of using scissors?

Notebook Reflection

What was the first thing you noticed after holding the magnifying glass on the string? About how many minutes passed before this first event occurred? How long in all did it take to actually "cut" the string.

How Do I Use Electricity?

Name _____

What You Need: • a timer

What To Do:

1. Your teacher will set the timer for five minutes.

2. Look around the room. Find the things that use electricity. Look for things that are plugged in.

3. Fill in the chart. Draw pictures of the things.

Thing	What does it do?	Where does it get its power?

4. Talk about the things that you found. Where do they get electricity from?

5. Add things that you missed to your chart.

6. Some things are not plugged in. But they use power. How? They run on batteries. Batteries _____ energy.

Circle one: give / use

 **Next Question**

Name three things in your home that use electricity. Draw them. Tell what they do.

 Notebook Reflection

What kinds of things run on electricity?

How Can I Light a Lightbulb?

Name _____

What You Need: • rubber balloons

• fluorescent light bulb

What To Do:

1. Darken the room as much as possible — the darker the room the better!

2. Rub the balloon on your hair as rapidly as possible for several seconds.

3. Touch the balloon to the light bulb. What happens?

4. What normally causes the light bulb to light up?

 **Next Question**

If you used different sized balloons in the experiment, would they make the light bulb light up for a longer amount of time? Why or why not?

 Notebook Reflection

How is this experiment like lightning?

How Can a Battery Make Heat?

Name _____

What You Need:
- 3 cm x 15 cm (1 in. × 6 in.) strip of foil
- AA battery
- timer

What To Do:

1. Fold the foil in half (hot dog style).

2. Fold the foil in half again (hot dog style). You have made a wire.

3. Hold the battery with one hand. With the other hand, hold the ends of the wire against the ends of the battery.

4. Hold the wire for 10 seconds. It feels _____ than before.

   Circle one: the same / colder / hotter

5. Quickly take the wire from the battery.

6. Batteries store electric energy. The wire let this energy flow from the battery. Why did the wire's temperature change?

   _____

   _____

   _____

 **Next Question**

Name three things in your home that use batteries. What do these things do?

 Notebook Reflection

Draw the setup for this experiment. Write what happened.

How Can a Fruit Make Electricity?

Name _____

What You Need:
- a lemon
- a copper coin (like a penny)
- a nickel coin (like a nickel)
- two pieces of electrical wire with the ends exposed (Have the teacher strip the ends for you.)
- a knife

What To Do:

1. The teacher makes two cuts, about an inch apart, in the lemon.

2. Take the coins and push each coin into one of the cuts. Push the coins almost all the way down.

3. Take one wire and push it all the way down next to the penny.

4. Take the other wire and push it all the way down next to the nickel.

5. Hold both ends of the wires and touch them to your tongue. Pay attention to what you feel.

 **Next Question**

What happens if you touch only one wire to your tongue? Why is that?

 Notebook Reflection

What other items do you use that require batteries? How is the closed electrical system (or electrical loop) made? Draw a picture of one of the items and its electrical system.

How Does a Flashlight Work?

Name _____

What You Need:
- flashlight
- fresh batteries
- electrical wire

What To Do:

1. Carefully take your flashlight apart and look at the parts.

2. Experiment with them. What do the parts do? How do they work together?

3. Draw what you find out:

4. Now reassemble the flashlight.

5. Does it work? Was it hard putting it back together?

_____

_____

_____

How Does a Flashlight Work? *(cont.)*

What To Do: *(cont.)*

6. Take the batteries and lightbulb from the flashlight and get some electrical wire. Find a way to make the lightbulb light up. Draw what you do:

Next Question

How could you make a better flashlight? Draw a diagram. Label the parts.

Notebook Reflection

Use words and drawings to explain how a flashlight works.

154 #50163—*Science Labs: Standards-Based Investigations—K–2* © *Shell Education*

What Is Sound Made Of?

Name _____

What You Need:
- a balloon
- music stereo
- plastic wrap
- rice
- bowl
- rubber band
- saucepan
- metal spoon

What To Do:

1. Find a partner.

2. Place your fingers against your throat. Start talking. What do you feel?

_____

_____

_____

3. Blow up the balloon and tie the end.

4. Hold the balloon in front of you. Move towards the stereo playing music. What can you feel?

_____

_____

_____

5. Use both hands to hold it against your ear. Ask your partner to talk normally to you. What do you hear?

_____

_____

_____

What Is Sound Made Of? *(cont.)*

What To Do: *(cont.)*

6. Now ask your partner to talk with their mouth against the balloon. Write about and draw what happens.

7. Stretch the plastic wrap across the mouth of the bowl. Use the rubber band to hold it in place.

8. Sprinkle a few grains of rice on top of the drum.

What Is Sound Made Of? *(cont.)*

What To Do: *(cont.)*

9. Hold the saucepan near the bowl and hit it with the spoon to make noise. Watch the rice. Record what happens.

10. Repeat step #9 with different noises. What happens?

	Sound	Effect
1		
2		
3		
4		
5		

Next Question

What makes the rice bounce the most? What can you do to make the rice bounce the most?

Notebook Reflection

Write about what you learned in the lab. What happened whenever there was sound?

How Is a Kazoo Made?

Name _____

What You Need:
- cardboard tube
- scissors
- wax paper
- rubber band
- ruler

What To Do:

1. Measure 4 cm (2 in.) in from one end of the cardboard tube. Make a mark.

2. Cut out a small circle at the mark.

3. Cut out a piece of wax paper and place it over the end of the cardboard tube.

4. Hold the wax paper in place with a rubber band.

5. Hold the other end of the tube to your mouth. Hum. Describe what happens.

_____

_____

_____

? Next Question

Fold a tissue paper over a comb. Hold it to your lips and hum. What happens?

Notebook Reflection

How could you make a whole band?

How Can I Make Noise?

Name _____

What You Need:
- cardboard tube
- funnel
- tape
- balloon

What To Do:

1. Blow up the balloon.

2. Hold the neck closed and slip the end of the balloon over the small end of the funnel.

3. Stretch the neck of the balloon as you let the air escape. Describe what happens.

_____

_____

_____

4. Tape the big end of the funnel to on end of the cardboard tube. Repeat steps #1–#3. Describe what happens.

_____

_____

_____

 **Next Question**

Experiment with different lengths of tube. What changes?

 Notebook Reflection

Describe what you think turns air into noise.

How Do Shadows Work?

Name _____

What You Need:
- 3 craft sticks
- construction paper
- scissors
- tape
- flashlight

What To Do:

1. Cut out a square, a circle, and a triangle from your construction paper.

2. Draw your shapes. Label them:

3. Get three craft sticks.

4. Tape each shape to a craft stick.

5. Turn off the lights.

6. Turn on your flashlight.

How Do Shadows Work? *(cont.)*

What To Do: *(cont.)*

7. Take the circle. Hold it between the flashlight and the wall. Draw its shadow:

How Do Shadows Work? (cont.)

What To Do: (cont.)

8. Take the triangle. Hold it between the flashlight and the wall. Draw its shadow. Do the same for the square:

9. A shape makes a shadow of _____ shape.

Circle one: the same / a different

 Next Question

How can you make the square's shadow smaller without cutting the square? How do you make the square's shadow bigger?

 Notebook Reflection

Describe how the light and the shadow are connected. Use words and drawings.

Forces and Motion

This chapter provides activities that address McREL Science Standard 10.

Student understands forces and motion.

Knows that magnets can be used to make some things move without being touched	How Can I Make a Magnet?, page 169 Is It Magnetic?, page 170 How Can I Make It Move?, page 171 How Can I Make It Fly?, see Teacher CD
Knows that things near the Earth fall to the ground unless something holds them up	How Fast Does It Fall?, page 173 How Can Air Make It Spin?, page 174 How Does It Roll?, page 177
Knows that the position of an object can be described by locating it relative to another object or the background	Where Is It?, page 179 Where Are They Now?, see Teacher CD
Knows that the position and motion of an object can be changed by pushing or pulling	How Much Pull Do I Need?, page 181 How Do Balloon Rockets Work?, page 182 How Do Balls Move?, page 183 How Does a Pulley Work?, see Teacher CD
Knows that things move in many different ways (e.g., straight line, zigzag, vibration, circular motion)	How Can I Make a Shoebox Guitar?, page 185 How Do Things Move?, page 186 What Can I Do with a Balloon Rocket?, page 188 What Do I Push, Pull, and Twist?, page 189 How Is Music Made?, see Teacher CD

How to Teach Forces and Motion

So What Are Forces?

Forces are behind everything that is happening around us. Forces make things happen.

You probably think this subject is difficult. You are quite right to fear getting too deeply into it because when you do, you will have to suspend your disbelief and your trust in common sense. Forces just don't behave as we would expect them to. Teaching forces is not easy!

Take these examples. Which of them would you think are true?

1. Two balls the same size dropped together from the top of the Leaning Tower of Pisa will both hit the ground at the same moment, even if one is a foam ball and the other is made from lead.

2. A bullet fired horizontally across a field from a gun, and an identical bullet dropped at the same moment from the barrel, will both hit the ground simultaneously.

3. When you sit on a table, it pushes back at you with an equal and opposite force.

4. There are two forces acting on a kicked football once it is in the air—the drag of the air and the downward pull of gravity.

5. The force of gravity is pulling you downward, but you are also pulling Earth towards you with your own force of gravity.

That's right—all of them are true.

Well, almost.

Position, Velocity, and Acceleration

One of the more obscure foundations of physics is position and its derivatives velocity and acceleration. It is very easy to overlook the simple proposition that things have positions, and those positions change. However, all of forces and motion requires this foundational understanding in order to actually work.

Position

Position is where an object is. That position cannot be measured absolutely—that is, there is no position that describes where the object "really is." Instead, position can only be measured relative to other objects. The blue block is three inches from the red block. The text stops a half-inch from the edge of the page.

Velocity

Velocity is the rate at which position changes. Students will probably be familiar with the idea of speed. Velocity is speed plus a direction: not 50 kph (31 mph), but 50 kph (31 mph) due east.

Acceleration

Acceleration is the rate at which velocity changes. Students may be familiar with the word accelerate, thinking that it means "speed up." However, acceleration is any change in velocity: speeding up, slowing down, or changing direction.

Pushes and Pulls

Forces are pushes and pulls. You can't escape forces—they are around you all the time.

How to Teach Forces and Motion *(cont.)*

When you are cycling, you need to push on the pedals to move forward. The ground is pulling on your tires to slow you down. The air is pushing in your face. If you stop pedalling, the ground and the air will slow you down until you come to a stop, but their forces keep working.

Attach a trailer on the back of the bike. Now you are pulling. Your force on the trailer is a pulling force. You push the pedals; the bike pulls the trailer! Stop cycling and try sitting still. Surely no forces are acting now? In fact, the force of gravity is pulling down on you. And the ground is pushing back.

The ground? Pushing? Yes, it has to. If the ground didn't push back, you would fall to the middle of Earth. So the ground pushes on your bike, and your bike pushes on you. Good thing, too. You don't want to disappear into Earth!

Faster and Slower

You use forces when you change speed. Hop on a scooter. First, you want to accelerate. Push off with your foot. The ground is pushing back at you and you're away! Want to go faster? It's no good just thinking about it. A bit of force is needed. Foot down, push again, and again. That's better. Now you are really rolling.

Lamppost ahead. Time to slow down. Push your foot to the ground. Slowing… whoops! Bit of a mistake there. The lamppost is still coming up. Brakes on. Put foot down and push backwards. Too late. Contact. Unfortunately, the lamppost pushed back just as hard as you pushed on it. It certainly stopped you.

Changing Direction

You can't change direction without a force, either. It might be the push and pull you give to the scooter handlebars.

It might be the push and pull you give to a steering wheel. It might be the twisting force you give to your leg as you jump sideways to catch a ball. (You can see the results of that force if you look at the soles of your shoes. Old shoes get a well-worn jumping-off spot.)

Isaac Newton, the great scientist, stated this as a law in 1687. He said that every object would remain still, or carry on moving in the same direction at a steady speed, unless forces acted on it. This is called Newton's first law of motion.

It doesn't matter whether it is speeding up, slowing down, or changing direction, you need forces for change! Forces make things change direction. Try bouncing a ball. It changes direction when it hits the ground or the wall. But the new direction can be predicted. Try rolling a ball against the wall and seeing which way it bounces off. What do you notice? You can predict the angle—especially if you are a good billiards player!

Two Special Forces

There are two special forces. They are also invisible. They don't need to touch an object. They can act on an object without touching it. They are magnetism and gravity.

Magnetism

Magnets exert forces. The forces act on magnetic materials. Some metals, like iron and steel, are magnetic but not all metals are magnetic. Magnetic metals can be attracted over a distance. Magnets can repel other magnets, too. They can push other magnets over a distance.

Gravity

Gravity works over a distance, as well. All objects have gravity. But for those

of us on Earth, the gravitational pull of Earth is the nearest and strongest by far. Earth's gravity holds us on the planet. If you drop something, it will always fall downward. Earth's gravity pulls it down.

Is Magnetism Magic?

Magnets are magical and mysterious—a sure winner with students. They are also excellent subjects for investigations. All you need are a few well-chosen questions.

How Is a Magnet Made?

A material like iron is made up of countless tiny bits, all of them magnets. Usually, these little bits are facing randomly, like people crowded into a room. When the iron is made magnetic, all the magnetic bits face the same way. It's as if you open a window at one end of the room, and everyone turns to face it.

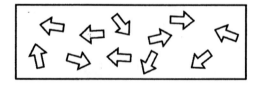

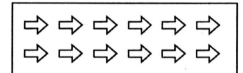

But heat a magnet, give it a good bashing, or let little Jimmy drop it on the classroom floor a few times, and all the magnetic bits will end up facing randomly again. Your magnet is weakened or destroyed. It's a good idea to put your magnets away with "keepers." These bridge the ends or poles of a pair of magnets and ensure that the magnetic force is circled and enclosed. Your magnets will last a lot longer if you do this!

Earth Is a Magnet

Four hundred years ago, a scientist named William Gilbert made a dramatic suggestion. He had looked at the way magnets turned to face north-south. This would happen, he argued, if Earth itself were a huge magnet.

He was right. Around every magnet there is an area, a field, where the invisible force of magnetism is operating. Earth has its own magnetic field. It has poles, just like any other magnet, which are not quite in the same places as the true north and south of Earth.

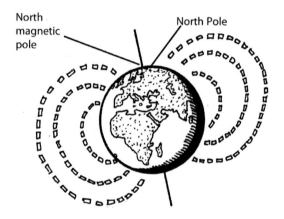

Electromagnets

The connection between electricity and magnetism was discovered in a classroom. In 1820, Hans Christian Oersted was teaching about electricity when he brought a magnetic compass close to the wire. To his amazement, the compass needle moved suddenly to line up with the wire. He realized that the electricity through the wire was making its own magnetic field.

There is a magnetic field around any wire that carries an electric current. Electromagnets have this wire coiled around a metal core. Electromagnets are magnets that can be switched on and off. When they are off, they are just iron bars inside a coil of insulated wire. When they are switched on, they become powerful magnets that can lift scrap metal, ring doorbells, and pull a steel splinter from your eye.

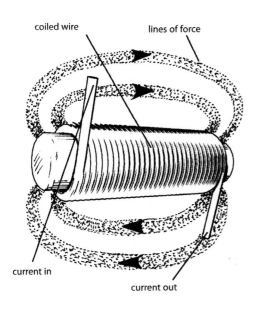

coiled wire
lines of force
current in
current out

Can a Magnet Make Electricity?

Electricity plus magnetism produces movement. And movement plus magnetism will produce electricity. If electricity flows through a wire, it produces magnetism and can move a magnet. And the reverse is true. If you move a magnet near a wire, then you generate electricity. You are doing just this if you have a dynamo-powered light on your bike. As you cycle along, you are providing the movement, and the moving magnets in the dynamo generate electricity for the bulb.

This was Michael Faraday's shattering discovery. Without this form of electricity generation, only batteries would provide our electricity. His invention changed the world. Electricity generators contain magnets. When you make the magnets move using a steam turbine, moving water, or the power of the wind, you generate electricity.

Gravity and the Apple Tree

We all dream that we could be as clever as the great scientist Sir Isaac Newton." If only an apple fell on my head," we think, "it would rattle my brain. I could have some brilliant ideas like him."

Bad news. The apple never fell on Newton's head.

Thousands of artists have drawn the apple conking poor old Isaac, and a light bulb lighting up. Idea! Now I can explain gravity.

Sadly, it wasn't like that. As Newton explained to a friend, he was walking in an orchard, puzzling over the problem of gravity, when an apple fell." Why does that apple fall downwards?" he thought. "Why does everything fall downward? It's as if there is a force pulling everything towards the center of Earth."

And there is. That force is gravity. It pulls everything towards the center of Earth. Everything has a force of gravity. The bigger it is, the bigger the force. But the biggest, nearest thing to you is Earth. Without gravity, nothing would stay on planet Earth that wasn't nailed down.

Earth's gravity is pulling down on us all the time. We call that pull your weight. You have weight because Earth's gravity is pulling down on your mass. The mass is the stuff you are made from. Your mass stays the same, wherever you are. But your weight can change.

If you went to another planet, the pull of gravity would change. If that planet were bigger than Earth, the pull would be stronger. If it were smaller than Earth, the pull would be weaker.

How to Teach Forces and Motion *(cont.)*

Can Heavy Things Fall Slowly?

Everyone finds it very hard to believe that light and heavy things, dropped together, can hit the ground together. Even when you've seen it, you may not believe it! Earth pulls harder on things of greater mass, and you might expect them to fall faster. But their greater mass means they're harder to get moving (just compare pushing a bicycle with push starting a car) and these two just about cancel each other out. Whatever the mass, objects fall at the same speed.

The exception, of course, is where one object has a greater surface area than another, catching the wind. A sheet of paper will float to the ground more slowly than a wadded-up ball; a feather will fall much more slowly than a hammer. The Moon astronauts graphically demonstrated what happens without the slowing effects of the air. A feather on the airless Moon dropped at the same speed as a hammer.

Balanced Forces

You can't see the forces acting on a football. They're invisible. One is the force of gravity. Gravity is pulling the ball down towards the center of Earth. So why doesn't the ball go down? Something is stopping it. The ground is pushing back on the ball. Gravity and the push of the ground are in balance. The ball stays where it is! When two forces are in balance, an object stays still. A space rocket on the launch pad has two forces acting on it—that of gravity pulling it down, and that of the launch pad pushing it up. These forces are in balance, and the rocket stays still. Until the engines start….

Floating and Sinking

Some objects float in liquids. Some sink. Some objects can be made to float, or they can be made to sink.

Objects float when they are lighter than the liquid. Even heavy objects can be made to float, as long as they are filled with air. The air makes them lighter than the liquid. When things are lighter than the liquid, the upthrust of the liquid holds them up. Gravity pulls down. The liquid pushes up. The two forces are in balance. The object stays still. It floats.

A floating object is in balance. The force of gravity is balanced by the upthrust of the liquid. As long as the object isn't too dense—when the force of gravity will exceed the upthrust of the liquid and the object will sink—the object will float, the forces on it nicely balanced.

When Are Forces Unbalanced?

When forces are unbalanced, things move. Take that space rocket. It is blasting off at John F. Kennedy Space Center. It is being held back by gravity, but gravity is a weak force compared to the tremendous thrust of the rocket engines. Because the forces are unbalanced, the rocket climbs into the sky.

When forces are unbalanced, things change shape. When you squeeze some modeling clay, the modeling clay pushes back. But if the modeling clay pushed back as hard as you squeezed, you could never change its shape.

How can I Make a Magnet?

Name _____

What You Need:
- a bar magnet
- paper clip
- clean sheets of paper

What To Do:

1. Carefully straighten out the two paper clips.

2. Take the bar magnet and rub it along each paper clip about twenty times.

3. Are the paper clips attracted to each other? _____

4. Try some magnetizing experiments!

   a. How many unmagnetized paper clips can the magnetic paper clip pick up? _____

   b. Can the magnetic paper clip move unmagnetized paper clips placed under a clean sheet of paper? _____

   c. Using two paper clips (one magnetized and one unmagnetized), challenge a classmate to a race! Use the magnetized paper clip to "pull" the unmagnetized paper clip a distance of one meter (one yard). Who can do this with the fastest speed?

 **Next Question**

What can you do to make the magnetized paper clip pick up more clips?

 Notebook Reflection

What would happen if everything you touched became magnetized?

Is It Magnetic?

Name _____

What You Need:

- magnets
- paper clips
- marbles
- nuts and bolts
- nails
- aluminum foil
- pebbles
- string
- blocks
- other metal and non-metal items
- scraps of paper

What To Do:

1. Using a magnet, test each object to see if it is magnetic or not.

2. Make a chart to record your results as each item is tested.

3. What did all of the magnetic items have in common? Which items were affected by the magnet? What happened when the magnet got near these items?

_____

_____

_____

_____

_____

_____

_____

Next Question

Write the directions for a magnetic trick. Share the trick with the rest of the class.

Notebook Reflection

Why do you think the paper clips, nuts and bolts, and nails were attracted to the magnet while the other items were not?

How Can I Make It Move?

Name _____

What You Need:
- paper plate
- bar magnet
- 3 steel ball bearings
- 2 thick books of equal size

What To Do:

1. Lay the books on your desk about 20 cm (8 in.) apart.

2. Set the paper plate on top of the books. Only the edges of the plate will be on the books. The plate must be flat.

3. Place the ball bearings on the paper plate.

4. Draw what you see:

5. Hold the bar magnet below the paper plate. Move it towards the ball bearings. Draw what happens.

How Can I Make It Move? *(cont.)*

What To Do: *(cont.)*

6. Turn over the bar magnet. Move it towards the ball bearings. Draw what happens.

7. Did the magnet touch the ball bearings?

_____

8. Can magnets make things move without touching them?

_____

 **Next Question**

Set the plate on your desk. Can the magnet make the ball bearings move through the desk and the plate? Why?

 Notebook Reflection

Forces make things push and pull. What did the magnet's forces do to the ball bearings?

How Fast Does It Fall?

Name _____

What You Need:
- wooden peg
- tape
- scissors

- 20 cm x 20 cm (8 in. x 8 in.) square of fabric
- four 20 cm (8 in.) pieces of string

What To Do:

1. Carefully stand on a chair.

2. Drop your square of fabric. Watch it fall.

3. Wrap the peg in the fabric. Tell your partner what you think will happen when you drop it. Now drop it.

4. Record your results.

   I thought this would happen: _____

   This is what did happen: _____

5. Tie a piece of string to each corner of the fabric. Tape the string ends to the peg. Tell your partner what you think will happen when you drop it. Now drop it.

6. Record your results.

   I thought this would happen: _____

   This is what did happen: _____

7. Cut a small hole in the middle of the fabric. Tell your partner what you think will happen. Then drop it again.

8. Record your results.

   I thought this would happen: _____

   This is what did happen: _____

 **Next Question**

Experiment with the materials. How can you make the peg and fabric fall even slower?

 Notebook Reflection

Imagine you went skydiving on vacation. Describe it. How is skydiving like the experiment?

How Can Air Make It Spin?

Name _____

What You Need: • paper   • scissors

What To Do:

1. Drop a piece of flat paper. Record what happens.

2. Fold the paper down the center, then unfold it. Drop it.
Record what happens.

How Can Air Make It Spin? *(cont.)*

What To Do: *(cont.)*

3. Fold the edges of the paper to meet at the center crease. Drop it. Record what happens.

4. Fold the two bottom corners up so the bottom edge meets the center crease. Drop it. Record what happens.

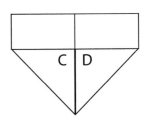

What To Do: *(cont.)*

5. Cut down the center crease from the top. Stop half-way.
   Drop it. Record what happens.

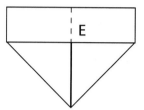

6. Fold the two top flaps in different directions. Drop it.
   Record what happens.

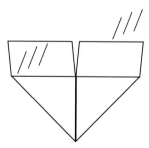

 **Next
Question**

*How can you make the paper
fall faster? Slower?*

 **Notebook
Reflection**

*Describe in words what
happened. Why do you think
the paper fell the way it did?*

How Does It Roll?

Name _____

What You Need:
- objects
- ramp
- newspaper
- butcher paper
- art paint (three colors)

What To Do:

1. Pick one object and let it go down the ramp. Watch it and record what you see below.

2. Repeat step #1 with two more objects.

 What To Do: *(cont.)*

3. Cover the ramp with white paper.

4. Place newspaper around the ramp, especially at the bottom.

5. Paint one side of an object. Let it go down the ramp.

6. Repeat step #5 with two more objects. Use different colors of paint on each one.

7. Use words to describe the three paths on the ramp paper.

_____

_____

_____

_____

 **Next Question**

How can you tell how an object will roll or slide? Test your idea.

 **Notebook Reflection**

Write how the objects' shapes change how they roll or slide.

Where Is It?

Name _____

What You Need:
- blocks of various shapes, sizes, and/or colors or various items or pictures of various items
- crayons or markers

What To Do:

1. With your teacher, brainstorm a list of words that tell where something is located. Write the words below.

_____

_____

_____

_____

2. Get in a group of four. Each student needs two blocks.

3. Take turns around the circle. When it is your turn, place a block on the table. Everyone should say one fact about the block's location. Write the facts down as you go.

_____

_____

_____

_____

Where Is It? (cont.)

What To Do: (cont.)

4. Draw the blocks as they are laid out.

Next Question

How would you describe the location of an item without using positional or directional words?

Notebook Reflection

Pick a shape and describe its location in several different ways. (Don't move the shape, just tell where it is using different positional words!)

How Much Pull Do I Need?

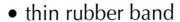

Name _____

What You Need:

- 2-liter plastic soda bottle
- 30 cm (1 ft.) of string
- ruler
- thin rubber band
- water

What To Do:

1. Tie the string around the bottle. Leave some length at the ends.

2. Tie the string to the rubber band.

3. Pull on the end of the rubber band until the bottle moves.

4. Still holding the rubber band taut, measure its length. How long is it? _____.

5. Fill the bottle with water.

6. Pull on the rubber band until the bottle moves.

7. Still holding the rubber band taut, measure its length. How long is it? _____.

8. The rubber band is ___ when pulling the bottle full of water.
   Circle One: longer / shorter

9. Pull the bottle across your desk. Is the bottle on the side of the desk where it started?

_____

 **Next Question**

Can you move the bottle without pushing or pulling it?

 Notebook Reflection

How can you change the position of an object?

How Do Balloon Rockets Work?

Name _____

What You Need:

- long balloons
- balloons of different sizes
- straw
- string
- paper
- stapler
- tape
- heavy sewing needle (optional)

What To Do:

1. Tape the middle of the paper to the straw.

2. Roll the paper and staple it to make a tube. Pinch one end of the tube closed and staple it that way.

3. Tie the string to something on one side of the classroom. Hold the other end and go to the other side of the classroom.

4. Thread the end of the string through the straw on your tube.

5. Have a partner hold the end of the string. Put a balloon inside your tube with the end dangling out. Blow up the balloon and then let it go.

6. Record what happens.

_____

7. Experiment with different balloons. Blow more or less air into them. Change your paper rocket around. What do you find out?

_____

_____

_____

? Next Question

What is the string for? What could you replace the string with?

Notebook Reflection

What do you think makes the paper rocket go?

How Do Balls Move?

Name _____

What You Need: • balls of different sizes

What To Do:

1. Choose one ball. Think about the different ways you make balls move in the games you play.

2. Draw what happens when you:

flick with finger	pat it

bowl it	bounce it

throw underarm

How Do Balls Move? (cont.)

What To Do: (cont.)

3. Pick another ball. Draw what happens when you:

flick with finger	pat it
bowl it	**bounce it**

throw underarm

 Next Question

Design a game that uses both kinds of balls. Players should move the balls in more than one way.

Notebook Reflection

Compare how the two different balls moved. What was different? What was the same?

How Can I Make a Shoebox Guitar?

Name _____

What You Need:
- shoebox
- 6 rubber bands of different widths and thicknesses

What To Do:

1. Take the lid off of the shoebox.

2. Stretch the rubber bands lengthwise around the shoebox. Leave about a 3 cm (1 in.) space between the rubber bands.

3. Pluck the strings to make beautiful music!

4. Order the strings so that the notes played go from high to low or low to high. What do you notice about the arrangement of the rubber bands?

_____

_____

_____

5. What can you do to make your guitar work differently?

_____

_____

_____

_____

? Next Question

Compare and contrast the shoebox guitar to a real guitar. How are they alike? How are they different?

Notebook Reflection

What force causes the guitar strings to make music? What other items use vibrations to make sounds?

How Do Things Move?

Name _____

What You Need:
- die-cast car
- top
- marble
- slinky

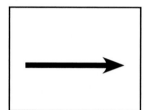   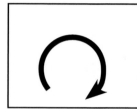

What To Do:

1. Find a partner.

2. When your teacher says "start," sing Yankee Doodle. Put one hand on your throat. Put your other hand on your partner's throat. Stop singing when your teacher tells you.

3. Draw the symbol from above that shows how your throat moves when you sing.

4. Push the car around your desk. Draw the ways that the car can move.

How Do Things Move? *(cont.)*

What To Do: *(cont.)*

5. Spin the top. How does it move?

_____

_____

6. Roll the marble around. Push it on your desk. Draw all the ways that the marble can move.

 Next Question

Make the slinky move in as many different ways as you can. Get a partner to hold on to one end of the slinky. Can you make it move in more ways with a partner's help?

Notebook Reflection

Copy the symbols for the different ways to move. Next to each one, list the things that moved that way. Think of two more things that move. Draw them next to each way that they can move.

What Can I Do with a Balloon Rocket?

Name _____

What You Need:
- string
- drinking straws
- two chairs
- tape
- toy car
- balloons of different sizes

What To Do:

1. Slide the straw onto a length of string.

2. Tie one end of the string to one chair and tie the other end of the string to the second chair.

3. Use tape to attach a balloon to the straw.

4. Blow up the balloon and hold the end closed with your fingers.

5. Release the balloon. What happens?

_____

6. Try these experiments with your rocket balloons:

a. Have a balloon race! See which balloon can travel the length of the string in the fasted time.

b. Devise a race course for the balloons. Do the balloons have enough rocket power to turn corners or go up an incline? _____

c. See which balloon can travel the longest distance.

d. Take this experiment a step further. Tape the balloon to the top of a toy car. Is the balloon able to move the car? _____

 **Next Question**

What would it be like to travel by rocket balloon instead of by car or by school bus?

 Notebook Reflection

Does the size or shape of the balloon impact how fast or how far the rocket balloons can travel?

What Do I Push, Pull, and Twist?

Name _____

What You Need: • plastic screw-top containers

What To Do:

1. Stand facing a friend, toe to toe. Gently push each other on the shoulder. What happens?

_____

2. What happens when you gently pull each other?

_____

3. Look around your classroom. What things can be pushed in or out? What things can be twisted?

_____

4. Try out some pushes, pulls, and twists. Draw what happens.

 **Next Question**

List which things were hard to push, pull, and twist. How are they similar? How are they different from the other things?

 Notebook Reflection

Think of the world around you. There are lots of pushes, pulls, and twists. List as many as you can.

References Cited

American Association for the Advancement of Science. 1989. Science for all Americans: A project 2061 report on literacy goals in science, mathematics, and technology.

American Association for the Advancement of Science. 1993. *Benchmarks for science literacy: Project 2061.* Oxford University Press.

Daniels, H., and S. Zemelman. 2004. Out with textbooks, in with learning. *Educational Leadership* (December 2003/January 2004):36–40.

Krueger, A., and J. Sutton. 2001. *EDThoughts: What we know about science teaching and learning.* Denver, CO: McREL.

Lemke, J. L. 1990. *Talking science: Language, learning, and values.* Westport, CT: Ablex.

National Academy of Science. National Science Education Standards. National Academy Press. http://www.nap.edu/readingroom/books/nses/.

Saul, E., ed. 2004. *Crossing borders in literacy and science instruction.* St Louis, MS: International Reading Association, Inc.

Their, M. 2002. *The new science literacy.* Portsmouth, NH: Heinemann.

Notes

Notes